AL-DAI AL-FATIMI
SYEDNA MOHAMMED BURHANUDDIN

AL-DAI AL-FATIMI

SYEDNA
MOHAMMED
BURHANUDDIN

An illustrated biography

AL-JAMEA-TUS-SAIFIYAH

Distributed by Oxford University Press

Al-Dai al-Fatimi, Syedna Mohammed Burhanuddin

A NOTE ON TRANSLITERATION

Transliterated terms adopted from the original Arabic are spelt using the widely accepted method approved by the Library of Congress with minor modifications. A full list of transliteration characters is provided at the end of the book. Some exceptions have been made, such as the words Syedna (*Sayyidnā*), al-Dai al-Mutlaq (*al-Dā'ī al-Muṭlaq*), Fatimi (*Fāṭimī* or *Fāṭimid*) and Dawoodi (*Dā'ūdī*). These and names of people have been treated in the way commonly used in the Dawoodi Bohra community. The Arabic article "al-" has been dropped when it is preceded by its English equivalent "the". In some cases, it has also been omitted from names such as al-Hasan and al-Husain to ease reading. Wherever Islamic and Gregorian dates have been written together, the Islamic date precedes the Gregorian one.

Al-Jamea-tus-Saifiyah
Badri Mahal,
211/213, Dr. D. N. Road
Fort, Mumbai 400 001
India

© Al-Jamea-tus Saifiyah 2001

First published in 2001
by Al-Jame'ah al-Saifiyah Trust
21 Gatehill Court, 166 Notting Hill Gate,
London W11 3QT

British Library Cataloguing-in-Publication Data
A catalogue record of this book is available from the British Library

ISBN 0-9536256-0-5

Text Mustafa Abdulhussein, NDI, PhD

Assistance Rashida Mustafa, MA, MA

Contributions Badrul Jamali Najmuddin, ZI, NDF
Dr. Idris Zainuddin, FJ, NDF, MBBS
Zainul Abedin Zainuddin, NDI, MA
Kinana Jamaluddin, FJ, MKD
Juzer Shakir, NKD, LLB
Shabbir Khumusi, FJ, NKD
Abdullah Shakir, FJ, NDI, BA

Photographs From the collection of the late rector of Al-Jamea-tus-Saifiyah.

Design and typesetting Karen Stafford

Printing and binding Silverpoint Press Pvt. Ltd., India

CONTENTS

Invocation

In the name of Allah, the Compassionate, the Merciful

All praise is for Allah. "There is no deity but He. He knows the hidden and the manifest. He is the Compassionate, the Merciful." "He comprehends and observes His servants." He sent His prophet, Mohammed, (unto mankind) as a witness, a bearer of glad tidings and as a warner; a resplendent light, permitted to summon mankind to Allah. Allah's peace and blessings be upon the Prophet unto whom He revealed the Qur'an "the like of which it is not possible for man and spirit together to reproduce". And who He made the seal of the prophets and the lord of the messengers. And this is indeed sufficient praise (of his qualities). And His peace and blessings be upon Ali, the brother of the Prophet, and his *waṣī* (successor), who He made the Prophet's equivalent in all angelic qualities except for prophethood; and through whom He strengthened the Prophet's aspirations and made him a sufficient aide and advisor. And His peace and blessings be upon their progeny, the *Ahl al-Bayt*, who He made innocent of all impurity, and to who are attributed the words of Allah "let there be from amongst you those who summon you towards good". And who Allah sustained with His power. And may this supplication bless the *du'āt muṭlaqīn* who, by the command of the *imām*, occupy the position of the *imām* who Allah has made the commander of the believers. They have, with the permission of the *imāms*, summoned the believers towards the haven of peace, giving them the good tidings of being recipients of a great boon from Allah. And upon the 51st amongst them, Syedna Taher Saifuddin, may he be showered with heavenly blessings. And upon the inheritor of all his excellent merits, the *dā'ī* of our time, Syedna Mohammed Burhanuddin. May Allah keep him amongst us and may his fragrant life remain ever fresh.

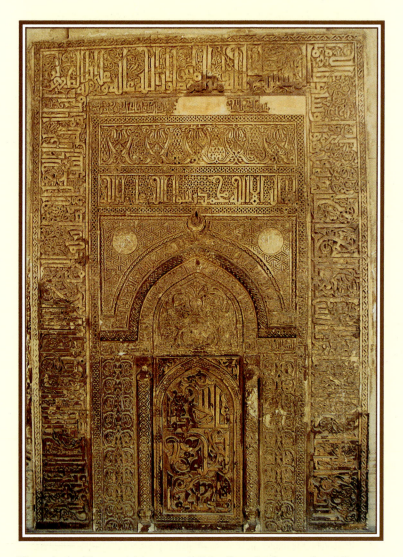

The *miḥrāb* of Imām al-Mustansir billah ﷺ in the famous Jāmiʻ Ibn Ṭūlūn in Cairo. Built in the 5th/11th century, it is rich in Fatimi script and design.

INTRODUCTION
Faith and historical legacy

Islam is a monotheistic religion based on a belief in divine guidance available to all human beings through a divinely appointed prophet. The function of a prophet, Islam teaches, is to convey the divine revelation. This revelation comprises of guidance, universal as well as specific, encompassing everything that is needed for humankind to reach its material and spiritual perfection. The prophet guides through his personal example, establishing the norms and rules for creating an ethical society on earth, which would lead humankind towards the purpose for which it was created.

The Qur'an, the message revealed to Prophet Mohammed ﷺ, speaks about a number of great prophets, common to Christianity and Judaism. The first such prophet was Adam ﷺ, who proclaimed the revealed message and called on people to affirm the Unity of God (*tawḥīd*) and to serve that one God, for prosperity in this life and salvation in the hereafter. These great teachers of humankind, which include Nuh (Noah) ﷺ, Ibrahim (Abraham) ﷺ, Musa (Moses) ﷺ and Isa (Jesus) ﷺ, challenged their contemporaries to rise above their petty interests and respond to the divine call, to work for the common good founded upon truth and justice. Thus from the beginning of human history with the first prophet, Adam ﷺ, to the last prophet, Mohammed ﷺ, the essential message taught by these prophets has remained one and the same, that is to worship none other than Allah, obey His instructions and follow the example of His prophets to build a just society.

Chronologically, of the three monotheistic religions based on a shared tradition of divine revelation, Judaism, Christianity and Islam, Islam is the last revealed and is therefore considered to complete the preceding messages, rendering its norms and principles final paradigms for all times. Prophet Mohammed ﷺ guided and nurtured a community of believers for twenty-three years (CE 610–632), and left the Qur'an and his close family, the Ahl al-Bayt, as two immutable sources of guidance that were to continue to provide salvational direction for his community, the *ummah*, after him.

Belief in the Ahl al-Bayt as the rightful successors of the Prophet and as guides of mankind is central to the faith of the Dawoodi Bohras. Their tradition, in common with all Shī'a Muslims, proclaims that Mohammed ﷺ was succeeded by his *waṣī* (legatee), Ali ibn Abi Talib ﷺ, who explained and interpreted the revelation received by Prophet Mohammed ﷺ. Ali ﷺ guided the Muslim community through his celebrated sermons and by leading a life of exemplary morality, courage, asceticism and forbearance. Ali ibn Abi Talib ﷺ, in turn, chose his sons Hasan ﷺ and Husain ﷺ as the first two *imāms* to continue to guide the community of believers.

It is an article of faith of the Dawoodi Bohras that such an *imām*, descended from the Prophet through his grandson, Imām Husain ﷺ, would always exist on earth to continue the mission of guiding mankind. Son succeeding father, the *imām*, like the Prophet, is believed to be sinless, inerrant, immaculate and sacred, the repository of prophetic knowledge, and the final interpreter of religion. History shows that such *imāms* protected the divine mission with great fortitude and sacrifice when adversities mounted. The second *imām*, Husain ☙, gave his own life and that of most of his loved ones in an epic battle to save the Muslim community and Islam itself from extinction. The third *imām*, Ali Zain al-Abidin ☙, wrote voluminous supplications that inspire the pious even today. Imām Ahmad al-Taqi ☙, the ninth *imām*, wrote the encyclopaedic *Rasā'il Ikhwān al-Ṣafā'* that aimed to demonstrate the supremacy of Qur'anic revelation over all the prevailing sciences and philosophies. The work rescued the 3rd/9th-century community from relinquishing the values of Islam and illumined the scholastic world for centuries.

The Fatimi Imāms

In this revered lineage were the ten Fatimi imām-caliphs who ruled an Islamic empire for over two hundred years commencing in the 4th/10th century. The eleventh *imām*, Abdullah al-Mahdi billah ☙, emerged from seclusion to found a state in North Africa and re-establish a society based on the teachings of the

The Imāms

1	Imam al-Hasan al-Zaki	d. 49/669	Madina, Saudi Arabia
2	Imam al-Husain al-Taqi	d. 61/680	Karbala, Iraq
3	Imam Ali Zain al-Abidin	d. 94/712	Madina, Saudi Arabia
4	Imam Mohammed al-Baqir	d. 114/732	Madina, Saudi Arabia
5	Imam Jafar al-Sadiq	d. 148/765	Madina, Saudi Arabia
6	Imam Ismail al-Wafi	—	Madina, Saudi Arabia
7	Imam Mohammed al-Shakir	—	Farghana, Iran
8	Imam Abdullah al-Radi	—	Salamiyya, Syria
9	Imam Ahmad al-Taqi	—	Salamiyya, Syria
10	Imam al-Husain al-Zaki	—	Askar Mukram, Iran
11	Imam Abdullah al-Mahdi	d. 322/934	Mahdiyya, Tunisia
12	Imam Mohammed al-Qaim	d. 334/946	Mahdiyya, Tunisia
13	Imam Ismail al-Mansur	d. 341/953	Mansuriyya, Tunisia
14	Imam Maad al-Moiz	d. 365/975	Cairo, Egypt
15	Imam Nizar al-Aziz	d. 386/996	Cairo, Egypt
16	Imam al-Husain al-Hakim	d. 411/1021	—
17	Imam Ali al-Zahir	d. 427/1036	Cairo, Egypt
18	Imam Maad al-Mustansir	d. 487/1094	Cairo, Egypt
19	Imam Ahmad al-Mustali	d. 495/1101	Cairo, Egypt
20	Imam Mansur al-Amir	d. 526/1132	Cairo, Egypt
21	Imam al-Tayyib		

Prophet. His successors protected the community and expanded the nascent territory until the celebrated fourteenth *imām*, Maad al-Moiz li-Dinillah 🕮, conquered Egypt and founded the city of Cairo in 358/969. From then on, Cairo was to be the capital of an empire that eventually included almost the whole of the Islamic world from North Africa to Arabia. During its zenith in the 5th/11th century, kingdoms as far away as the present day Pakistan offered allegiance to the *imām*.

Adopting their name from their ancestor Fatima 🕮, the daughter of Prophet Mohammed 🕮 and the wife of Ali 🕮, the Fatimi *imām*s ruled with the aim of fostering and strengthening the religious traditions established by the Prophet. In the process, they encouraged thoughts and philosophies that nourished a civilisation and founded educational establishments such as al-Azhar, the world's oldest surviving university, and Dār al-'Ilm. The *imām*s were great patrons of the arts and architecture, attracting the Islamic world's finest scientists and artists to their empire and building numerous edifices dedicated to worship and to learning. They nurtured a society of tolerance in which Muslims of different schools of thought and non-Muslims alike could practice their faith in a freedom that was rare in these historical periods.

Their *dāʿ*ī*s* (summoners to faith), many in number, spread throughout the land as emissaries, missionaries and governors, and excelled in all spheres of life. Great minds such as Syedna Abu Yaqub al-Sijistani 🕮, Syedna Jafar ibn Mansur al-Yaman 🕮, Syedna al-Qadi al-Numan 🕮, Syedna Hamiduddin al-Kirmani 🕮 and Syedna al-Muayyad al-Shirazi 🕮, wrote hundreds of works of Qur'anic exegesis, theology, philosophy, jurisprudence and poetry in an efflorescence that continues to feed the keen mind even after a millennium. Thus, the reign of the Fatimi *imām*s was one of the most brilliant periods of Islamic history in terms of its political, economic, literary, artistic and scientific achievements.

The seclusion of the Imām

It is a fundamental principle in the faith of the Dawoodi Bohras that an *imām*, from the progeny of the Prophet must, of necessity, continue to exist on earth. If he deems it necessary, however, an *imām* may choose to remain secluded from society and provide guidance from seclusion. In the 3rd/9th century, the 7th to 10th *imām*s chose to retire from public view and allowed their *dāʿ*ī*s* to operate on their behalf. Similarly, in 526/1132, the 21st *imām*, al-Tayyib 🕮, chose complete seclusion and since then all *imām*s, each appointed by his father and predecessor, has done likewise. It is through belief in this line of succession that the Dawoodi Bohras are said to belong to the Shīʿa Fāṭimī Ismāʿīlī Ṭayyibī branch of Islam.

As the time for seclusion neared, the 20th *imām*, Mansur al-Amir bi-Ahkamillah 🕮, instructed his grand emissary, Sayyida Arwa bint Ahmad 🕮, the queen of Yemen, to vest in the office of al-Dai al-Mutlaq, the vicegerency of the *imām* when the *imām* enters seclusion. During the seclusion of the *imām*, the bearer of the office was to continue the mission of the *imām*, known as *al-Daʿwah al-Hādiyah* (also Dawat-e-Hadiyah) literally, the rightly guiding mission, providing salvational guidance to believers. Each al-Dai al-Mutlaq (literally, summoner with comprehensive authority) was to preserve the faith up to the *imām's* return, guide the faithful of his time and appoint his successor just as the *imām* in seclusion, appoints his. The *dā'ī* was to act as deputy to the *imām*, lead with the authority of the *imām* and his pronouncements were to be regarded by his believers as being the same as the *imām's*. He was to keep the community together as one entity and ensure the purity of the fellowship. For his followers, faith in his spiritual mission was to be an essential part of their creed.

The Dā'īs

The first *dā'ī*, Syedna Zoeb ibn Musa al-Wadii 🕮, was appointed in 532/1138 in Yemen. By this time, the community of believers had become comparatively small in number, residing almost entirely in Yemen and India. They were no longer part of a flourishing empire calling others to their faith, but a minority group practicing their faith in solitude. Isolated from the hub of historical movements in the Northern Middle East, they were neither the direct beneficiaries of the affairs of the Islamic world, nor victims of its calamities.

Twenty-three *dā'īs* operated from their mountain bases in Yemen for over four centuries. Despite the turbulence of the times, having to face the onslaught of persecuting armies, the *dā'īs* persevered in their mission to lead the faithful and preserve the faith. They diligently taught their followers and wrote profusely to elaborate upon and elucidate the knowledge bequeathed to them by the *imām*s. The 3rd *dā'ī*, Syedna Hatim Muhyiddin 🕮, for example, was an accomplished scholar and an inspired writer and orator who consolidated the community at a critical period. The 19th *dā'ī*, Syedna Idris Imaduddin 🕮, wrote numerous works, including a complete history of the Fatimi faith.

In India, a sizeable community of followers had existed since the 5th/11th century, even before the seclusion of the *imām*. After seclusion, they remained loyal to the *dā'īs* in Yemen and the more eminent among them used to visit Yemen and stay with the *dā'īs* for long periods, obtaining first-hand knowledge of the traditions of their faith and observing how the affairs of the community were managed. The *dā'īs* in Yemen also appointed representatives (*wālīs*) in India who attended to the affairs of the community in India. Eventually, the devotion of the followers in India made the transfer of the seat of the Dawat to India inevitable. In 946/1539, Syedna Yusuf Najmuddin 🕮 of Sidhpur, India, was chosen as the 24th *dā'ī*, and with him, the seat of the Dawat moved to India, where it has remained to this day. The Bohras, so known because they comprised a predominantly trading community, (the name comes from the Gujarati word for "trader"), began to be known as Dawoodi Bohras in the 11th/16th century after their 27th *dā'ī*, Syedna Dawood ibn Qutubshah Burhanuddin 🕮.

The *dā'īs* bore the responsibility of office through the centuries in a spirit of dedication to the *imām*. When it became necessary for the protection of the mission of the *imām* and the wellbeing of their followers, they bore hardships of imprisonment and banishment, the 32nd *dā'ī*, Syedna Qutubkhan

The Dā'īs
during the seclusion of the Imām

1	Syedna Zoeb ibn Musa al-Wadii	d.546/1151	Hus, Yemen
2	Syedna Ibrahim ibn al-Husain al-Hamidi	d.557/1162	Ghayl Bani Hamid, Yemen
3	Syedna Hatim Muhyiddin al-Hamidi	d.596/1199	al-Hutayb, Yemen
4	Syedna Ali ibn Hatim al-Hamidi	d.605/1209	Sanaa, Yemen
5	Syedna Ali ibn Mohammed al-Walid	d.612/1215	Haraz, Yemen
6	Syedna Ali ibn Hanzala	d.626/1229	Hamdan, Yemen
7	Syedna Ahmad ibn al-Mubarak	d.627/1230	Sanaa, Yemen
8	Syedna al-Husain ibn Ali	d.667/1268	Sanaa, Yemen
9	Syedna Ali ibn al-Husain	d.682/1284	Sanaa, Yemen
10	Syedna Ali ibn al-Husain	d.686/1287	Sanaa, Yemen
11	Syedna Ibrahim ibn al-Husain	d.728/1328	Hisn Afida, Yemen
12	Syedna Mohammed ibn Hatim	d.729/1329	Hisn Afida, Yemen
13	Syedna Ali Shamsuddin ibn Ibrahim	d.746/1345	Zamarmar, Yemen
14	Syedna AbdulMuttalib ibn Mohammed	d.755/1354	Zamarmar, Yemen
15	Syedna Abbas ibn Mohammed	d.779/1378	Hisn Afida, Yemen
16	Syedna Abdullah Fakhruddin	d.809/1407	Zamarmar, Yemen
17	Syedna al-Hasan Badruddin	d.821/1418	Zamarmar, Yemen
18	Syedna Ali Shamsuddin	d.832/1428	Shariqa, Yemen
19	Syedna Idris Imaduddin	d.872/1468	Shibam, Yemen
20	Syedna al-Hasan Badruddin	d.918/1512	Masar, Yemen
21	Syedna al-Husain Husamuddin	d.933/1527	Masar, Yemen
22	Syedna Ali Shamsuddin	d.933/1527	Masar, Yemen
23	Syedna Mohammed Izzuddin	d.946/1539	Zabid, Yemen
24	Syedna Yusuf Najmuddin	d.974/1567	Tayba, Yemen
25	Syedna Jalal Shamsuddin	d.975/1567	Ahmedabad, India
26	Syedna Dawood Burhanuddin ibn Ajabshah	d.999/1591	Ahmedabad, India
27	Syedna Dawood Burhanuddin ibn Qutubshah	d.1021/1612	Ahmedabad, India
28	Syedna ShaykhAdam Safiyuddin	d.1030/1621	Ahmedabad, India
29	Syedna AbdulTayyib Zakiyuddin	d.1041/1631	Ahmedabad, India
30	Syedna Ali Shamsuddin	d.1042/1632	Hisn Afida, Yemen
31	Syedna Qasimkhan Zainuddin	d.1052/1642	Ahmedabad, India
32	Syedna Qutubkhan Qutbuddin	d.1056/1646	Ahmedabad, India
33	Syedna Pirkhan Shujauddin	d.1065/1655	Ahmedabad, India
34	Syedna Ismail Badruddin	d.1085/1674	Jamnagar, India
35	Syedna AbdulTayyib Zakiyuddin	d.1110/1699	Jamnagar, India
36	Syedna Musa Kalimuddin	d.1122/1710	Jamnagar, India
37	Syedna Nur Mohammed Nuruddin	d.1130/1718	Mandvi, India
38	Syedna Ismail Badruddin	d.1150/1737	Jamnagar, India
39	Syedna Ibrahim Wajihuddin	d.1168/1754	Ujjain, India
40	Syedna Hibatullah al-Muayyad Fiddin	d.1193/1779	Ujjain, India
41	Syedna AbdulTayyib Zakiyuddin	d.1200/1785	Burhanpur, India
42	Syedna Yusuf Najmuddin	d.1213/1798	Surat, India
43	Syedna AbdeAli Saifuddin	d.1232/1817	Surat, India
44	Syedna Mohammed Izzuddin	d.1236/1821	Surat, India
45	Syedna Tayyib Zainuddin	d.1252/1837	Surat, India
46	Syedna Mohammed Badruddin	d.1256/1840	Surat, India
47	Syedna AbdulQadir Najmuddin	d.1302/1885	Ujjain, India
48	Syedna AbdulHusain Husamuddin	d.1308/1891	Ahmedabad, India
49	Syedna Mohammed Burhanuddin	d.1323/1906	Surat, India
50	Syedna Abdullah Badruddin	d.1333/1915	Surat, India
51	Syedna Taher Saifuddin	d.1385/1965	Mumbai, India
52	Syedna Mohammed Burhanuddin		

Qutbuddin 🌸, even laying down his life. Being a minority, the Bohra community was often subject to persecution by petty rulers who thrived on religious differences. A puritanical movement could ignite local rivalries and cause severe persecution and the martyrdom of many.

The 51st *dā'ī*, Syedna Taher Saifuddin 🌸, led the community through the first half of the 20th century. An accomplished scholar, a prolific writer and poet, a skilful administrator and a man of vision, he re-vitalised the community, fostered strong faith, modernised the organisation of the Dawat, promoted welfare and education in the community and guided it sagaciously through the tumultuous period of world wars and independence of nations.

Thus, the *dā'ī*s have, in the last nine centuries, played a central role in moulding the lives of the Dawoodi Bohras. They have been the community's guides, patriarchs and paradigms of a Fatimi way of life. Their piety and disciplined life, erudition and scholarship, judicious guidance and leadership have upheld the sanctity of the office of al-Dai al-Mutlaq. By making difficult decisions with a firmness that comes only through deep belief in their cause, they steered the community through difficult periods, which at times threatened its very existence. This assured leadership has united the Dawoodi Bohras and given them a sense of direction, a sense of culture and tradition and a sense of belonging to a faith and an integrated community, that has been its main strength throughout its history.

Syedna Mohammed Burhanuddin

It is to this historic office of al-Dai al-Mutlaq that Syedna Mohammed Burhanuddin 🌸, also known as al-Dai al-Fatimi, is 52nd incumbent. His period in office began in 1385/1965, and has seen an efflorescence in the community's sense of purpose and dedication to faith. The faith which Syedna embodies is based upon the belief in one deity, Allah, in the Qur'an as the Word of Allah, and in the sacred mission of the prophets and their successors, the *imāms*. It requires adherence to religious practice as defined by the Islamic *sharī'ah*. It obligates a moral and disciplined life that makes binding the pursuit of a life in the hereafter through knowledge and good deeds. This, in turn, establishes a way of life in which the individual, the family, societal systems and the ethical mores of each, cohere in a single spiritual aim.

The thirty-five year era of Syedna has been one of fulfilment and progress for his community. The capacity to grow in faith has been evoked and fostered. Venerated practices have been reaffirmed and harmonised with contemporary exigencies and the moral, spiritual and mental equipment necessary to lead a meaningful life in the 21st century have been forged.

Acknowledgements

To understand a visionary is tantamount to having a vision oneself. A man of vision often acts beyond, or contrary to, common expectation. He perceives and acts according to his vision even when none can see its value. As the results of his foresight become noticeable over time, and the truth of his intuition gradually becomes clearer, the observer begins to fathom the depth of understanding that had been required to perceive the original vision with such clarity.

Thus, when Al-Jamea-tus-Saifiyah decided to render aspects of the life of Syedna Mohammed Burhanuddin 🌼 to record, they were faced with the task of having to order the achievements of his lifetime without forcing a fragmentation on the holism of the endeavour. This might not have been possible at all if Syedna had not himself spoken of the movements he had initiated during the thirty-five years of leadership of his community, that provided a definition of his life's work.

Al-Jamea-tus-Saifiyah is thankful for being able to publish this as a token of their indebtedness to a leader who has continuously sought to raise the standards of the academy. His personal devotion to the education of the students of the academy and his concern for their wellbeing has for years, profoundly affected every student and teacher. Their prayer that Allah bestows the best of His grace on Syedna Mohammed Burhanuddin 🌼 is, it is hoped, expressed in this tribute.

The academy gratefully acknowledges the support of Shahzada Idris Badruddin and the efforts of all of the many devoted commentators, reviewers and calligraphists who have contributed to this publication.

A graphic rendering of the "Verse of Light" in stone. Light symbolizes
the knowledge that illumines the soul. Al-Aqmar, Cairo.

AN EDUCATIONAL ENDEAVOUR

فَقُمْ بِعِلْمٍ وَلَا تَبْغِ بِهِ بَدَلًا

فَالنَّاسُ مَوْتَى وَأَهْلُ الْعِلْمِ أَحْيَاءُ

'Occupy yourself in the seeking of knowledge

without let, for only the knowledgeable are truly alive.'

AMĪR AL-MU'MINĪN ALI IBN ABI TALIB

'Like the dew, so minute in the face of rain,
even a little knowledge properly imbibed and
assimilated, does a great deal of good.'

SYEDNA MOHAMMED BURHANUDDIN

AN EDUCATIONAL ENDEAVOUR

AL-DAI AL-FATIMI, Syedna Mohammed Burhanuddin 🌼, is heir to a remarkable tradition of learning. He is a repository of knowledge that is divine in origin and represents a philosophy of education that has traversed the span of history.

The Prophet Mohammed al-Mustafa 🌼 made the seeking of knowledge compulsory for every Muslim man and woman. Knowledge ('ilm) is regarded as sacred; the act of seeking and acquiring it as a cause of merit and forgiveness, and the interaction between the teacher and the student as one that attracts celestial protection and grace. Except for the acknowledgement of Allah, His messengers, and the efficacy of His revelations, there is no obligation in Islam more important, more indispensable and more beneficial than the injunction to acquire knowledge and impart learning.

Such is the position of knowledge and education in Islam, that the word Islam, for centuries, was synonymous with knowledge. This tradition impelled a civilisation that saw all forms of learning flower upon an epistemology soundly rooted in the Islamic value-system. Sciences and philosophies developed under the firm belief of a created purposeful universe and mankind's technological and social progress was based upon a moral and ethical system founded on Islam. In this milieu, the Fatimi empire, headed by the *imām* from the progeny of the Prophet, excelled and bequeathed to posterity its rich philosophy of education and noble legacy of knowledge. Unfortunately the vicissitudes of time and historical circumstance caused the classical Islamic civilisation to wane and the larger body of Muslims entered the 20th century with few of these qualities.

Each *dā'ī* has, however, during the seclusion of the *imām*, preserved and enriched the tradition of education and learning that was once the essence of a civilisation. Syedna Mohammed Burhanuddin 🌼 is now the custodian of this tradition, and like his predecessors, articulates the spirit of revelation that is within the Qur'an. He considers it his duty to expound the learning of the *imām*s to all those who seek it. Tracing his authority, status and insight to their impeccable example, he has the task of restoring to his community, the philosophies and approach to education that once created an entire civilisation.

To facilitate this, he has fostered a renewed zeal and ardour in education by creating educational establishments that incorporate the traditional approaches to education with the best that contemporary education has to offer. Al-Jamea-tus-Saifiyah, in Surat and Karachi, both full-fledged academies, epitomise this orientation, as do many schools of primary and secondary education throughout the Bohra world. He supervises the curricula and ensures that the best attention and effort is made available to this endeavour. At a more personal level, he writes treatises that form a treasury of knowledge. Moreover he has facilitated the transmission of his *wa'z* (discourses) so that hundreds of thousands benefit from his erudition directly.

This ongoing process of education is to be viewed as a movement on which the value-system of future generations is to be built. It is, as Syedna has often said, a critical and priceless process.

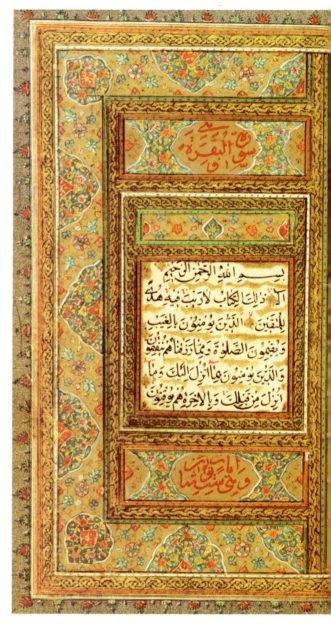

The all-encompassing importance that the Qur'an gives to learning and knowledge to those who live by its message is threaded through the entirety of its pages. This is underscored by the fact that the first words revealed to the noble Messenger, the Prophet Mohammed ﷺ were to ask the Messenger and through him, the whole of mankind, to "Read".

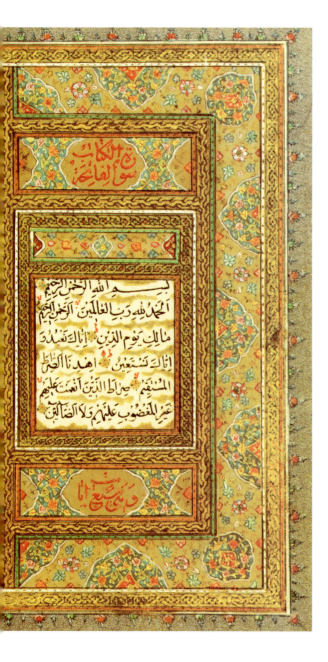

'Read in the name of your Lord
who created.
Created man from a clot of
congealed blood.
Read! And your Lord is Bounteous,
who taught by the Pen.
Taught man that which he did not
know.'

AL-QUR'AN 96:1–5

'The Qur'an quenches the thirst of a scholar.
It is the delight of learned men.
It is a spring of knowledge and its ocean.
It is a clear path for the virtuous.'

AMĪR AL-MU'MINĪN ALI IBN ABI TALIB

"The Qur'an", says Syedna, "uplifts the believer to the heights of nobility and leadership and elevates him to the world of purity and perpetuity". The Qur'an is a miracle and its effects miraculous. Its words elevate the soul. Its language is pure and its Message untainted. It is the basis of all understanding of the philosophy of knowledge in Islam.

Syedna urges his followers to make it a practice to recite the Qur'an daily. He has reinforced many traditional practices that aid this, including public recitations after morning prayers.

He has encouraged the age-old tradition of committing the entire Qur'an to memory, having done so himself at an early age. Each year, many students carefully and meticulously complete the memorisation of the Qur'an and imbibe its every word, and thousands of children come before Syedna annually in Surat, India, to recite the chapters they have memorised.

The dissemination of religious and philosophical knowledge in the community follows the time-tested method of *sabaq*. The student sits with the teacher, establishes a personal rapport with him, and imbibes his mentor's knowledge step by step with humility, going beyond the written word. This traditional method, used by sages throughout history, still practiced by Syedna, and with his authority by other learned men and women, involves meticulously following each sentence and word of the Qur'an and other books of religion that interpret it.

The *wa'z*, a discourse delivered in a gathering that can be of thousands, is an educational experience as well as an act of worship. Here, a varied audience benefits from the community's theological heritage without distinctions of age, education or experience.

*'Four things are imperative for every
Muslim of intellect and sagacity. These are
to listen to knowledge with diligence, to
remember it, to act in conformity with it
and to propagate it.'*

MOHAMMED RASULULLAH ﷺ

The Legacy Of Knowledge

Allah places knowledge within creation for man to observe, deliberate upon, and imbibe. It is one of the greatest gifts of Allah to humankind. The purpose of this knowledge is to enable man to know the existence of his Maker and to instil in him an awe of the Creator and nearness to Him. Any knowledge that fails to do so is simply incorrectly imbibed or only partially understood. This is a Fatimi philosophy of knowledge. Whilst man is free to observe creation and understand his place within it, Allah also reveals His knowledge to His chosen messengers and prophets and guides mankind through them. To Prophet Mohammed ﷺ, He bestowed the last revelation, the Qur'an, vouchsafed all knowledge for him, and with him completed His favour to humankind.

It is an article of faith that revealed knowledge is always held, in its original form and in its interpretative value, in each age, by one chosen by Allah for that purpose, and that this knowledge, in its purity, encompasses all that can ever be known by man either through reason or application. The knowledge thus received by the Prophet was inherited by his successor, Ali ibn Abi Talib and was then transferred from father to son, *imām* after *imām*, each *imām* in his age being the impeccable repository of a divine knowledge and a learning tradition that is the essence of Islam.

As the vicegerent of the *imām* in seclusion, the *dā'ī* inherits this divine knowledge and teaches by this historic tradition. Over the last nine centuries, each *dā'ī* has carried out the exacting duty of spreading the knowledge of the *imām*s in individual and specialised ways, by writing books, delivering sermons, conducting classes and painstakingly shaping the life of his followers in the pursuit of the elevation of the soul. Syedna's own educational efforts are an extension of this epistemological system.

Al-Jamea-tus-Saifiyah, is an academy in Surat, founded by the 43rd *dā'ī*, Syedna AbdeAli Saifuddin in 1229/1814 where students are taught the intricacies of Islamic lore, classical Arabic literature and contemporary subjects in an integrated Islamic educational approach. It represents an educational movement and the learning tradition of the Fatimi *imām*s founders of the world's oldest university, Al-Azhar. This movement was subsequently preserved by the *dā'ī*s who created centres of education in Yemen and India, to which the faithful flocked.

The Academy's crest symbolises its position as an offspring of Fatimi culture. A verse from the Qur'an, a saying of the Prophet and the words of the 51st *dā'ī*, Syedna Taher Saifuddin, that encapsulate the Fatimi philosophy of knowledge are set within an arch derived from a portal of a Fatimi *masjid* in Cairo, al-Aqmar. The quotations affirm that all knowledge has a divine origin and that man receives knowledge through piety and worship.

Al-Jamea-tus-Saifiyah runs a curriculum lasting eleven years. Students are taught the Qur'an, Arabic language and literature, Islamic jurisprudence, history, philosophy and doctrine. Memorisation of the Qur'an and the learning of Arabic literature is given particular emphasis and the students' morality and piety are continuously evaluated. Along with the religious course, English, philosophy, psychology, and the social and natural sciences are also taught. The degrees conferred are *mubtaghī al-'ilm*, on successful completion of the first four years of study, *al-faqīh* on completion of seven years, *al-faqīh al-mutqin* on completion of nine years and *al-faqīh al-jayyid* at the end of eleven years. During the course of their study, they are often sent to different towns to lead the local communities, especially during Ramaḍān and Muḥarram.

The academy's architecture, such as in this building reflects its Islamic character, the Fatimi ethos of its education system as well as its contemporary situation. The academy's *masjid* with its minaret is to the right of a garden, the library is in the centre and the girls' hostel on the left.

The academy is a residential campus, with boarding and lodging provided. A tradition of the *dā'īs* has been to feed at their cost, the aspirants of knowledge. This tradition continues to this day and Mawā'id Sayfiyyah, where the students of Al-Jamea dine, articulates the etiquette and manners that epitomise the esteem in which scholarship is held.

One of the unique features of the Al-Jamea-tus-Saifiyah is its centre for the memorisation of the Qur'an, called Mahad al-Zahra. The first of its kind in the Islamic world, it was built with the specific intent of facilitating the memorisation of the words of revelation that have changed the course of mankind. This age-old practice is highly revered in Islam and the skill sharpens the mind and makes it more receptive to learning. The centre makes use of the latest technology and educational techniques to aid the memorisation process, including rooms that are designed to alter acoustic feedback. It has a serene atmosphere enhanced by internal gardens allowing memorisation to take place in a tranquil environment.

Al-Jamea-tus-Saifiyah is famed for its extensive library which is home to some of the rarest Islamic manuscripts, carefully preserved over a millennium. The manuscript library has given the academy the reputation of being a treasury of Arabic literature. Copies of these manuscripts are used in the daily instruction of the students.

A significant part of the library is organised in sections, each section or *zāwiyah* representing a meeting of walls, as occur in a corner, or a conglomeration of views, an understanding of different authors or a place of contemplation. The central *zāwiyah* is that of the Qur'an, signifying the central position of revelation within the body of knowledge. The library also houses some of the oldest and most exquisite manuscripts of the Qur'an. Seen below is Syedna examining one such manuscript during the opening of Mahad al-Zahra in December 1998.

Al-Jamea-tus-Saifiyah's integrated educational approach requires the availability of modern educational equipment and aids. Traditional mores combine with modern amenities and methods to provide a unique blend of education.

The students of Al-Jamea-tus-Saifiyah, boys and girls numbering about seven hundred, study for 11 years and imbibe an Islamic character that reflects their faith. In recent years, Syedna has greatly enhanced the academy, improved its stature and modernised its facilities and curriculum. Today Al-Jamea-tus-Saifiyah is the community's greatest resource for knowledge. Its graduates provide the community with its learned scholars and dedicated workers.

'In a critical study of the sum-total of the scientific and technical progress of the modern world, we must not undermine its achievements, nor deny its merits. Yet, we should not be overwhelmed by it. We must expose all the learning of science, technology, art and culture to a severe selective process so that we are well equipped for our journey of ultimate realisation. This is the crux of the teachings of (the 1200 year old) *Rasā`il Ikhwān al-Ṣafā`* when they said thus:

"It behoves our brethren, may Allah guide them, that they should not be against any type of knowledge, they should not reject any book, they should not bear intolerance for any religion. Our faith embraces all schools of thought and our knowledge encompasses all other knowledge."

Our predecessors and spiritual leaders, by precept and practice, have shown us the way we should proceed onwards; taught us to interact amicably with other religions, social and racial groups and seek their cooperation in our endeavours and create an atmosphere of mutual confidence whilst holding fast to our own tenets and faith.'

SYEDNA MOHAMMED BURHANUDDIN

Contrary to popular stereotyping, Islam does not diminish the importance of women's education. The Prophet made the seeking of knowledge obligatory upon Muslim men and Muslim women equally, and without distinction. Thus, women's education and women's involvement in the educational process of the community is given particular importance.

The girls' hostel, Rabwat Jiblah, maintains the privacy required by Islamic norms whilst providing it the most modern of amenities. It is named after a mountain from which the famous 12th century Queen of Yemen ruled. The queen, Sayyida Arwa bint Ahmad, is one of the most powerful role-models for women in the Dawoodi Bohra community, not only as an important political figure who played a vital role during a critical juncture in their history, but also for the vastness of her learning.

A second campus of Al-Jamea-tus-Saifiyah was built by Syedna Mohammed Burhanuddin in 1983 in Karachi, Pakistan. It trains about 400 boys and girls and follows an identical curriculum to the academy in Surat. Its buildings comprise a *masjid*, a library, an *īwān* (ceremonial hall) where examinations are held, classes, administrative rooms, hostels and sports facilities. It also takes pride in having a garden that includes trees for every fruit mentioned in the Qur'an.

The annual examinations of the academy are unique. They commence with a discourse by Syedna that sets the tone of the exams to follow and by extension, the entire year's educational focus for the whole community. Known as the *zikrā majlis*, the discourse is attended by Dawoodi Bohras from all over the world who stay on for the oral examinations, in which each student comes before the rectors of the academy for testing. Syedna oversees the examinations from a room above the examination hall, assigns marks to each student and supervises the process.

Seen here are views of the oral examinations, being taken by the four rectors of the academy, Shahzada Qasim Hakimuddin, Shahzada Abbas Fakhruddin, Shahzada Qaidjoher Ezzuddin and Shahzada Mufaddal Saifuddin (ABOVE and BELOW). The late Shahzada Dr. Yusuf Najmuddin is seen conducting the examinations as the rector of the academy, a position he occupied until his demise in 1987 (RIGHT).

Islamic Education

Allah is the source of all knowledge. This fundamental belief introduces a natural definition of Islamic education. By this definition any knowledge that leads one to develop an awareness of Allah and to the affirmation of His existence, His compassion and mercy, is knowledge that is inherently Islamic. Whether that knowledge is classified as an art or a science, or whether it is philosophical or empirical in nature, all of it is considered Islamic provided the principle of source and purpose is acknowledged. Thus, Islamic education is the pursuit of any and all knowledge with the ultimate purpose of understanding the mysteries of creation in contemplation of the existence of the Creator. An Islamic educational program based on this definition should necessarily cater for all the needs of the human being, whether that need is spiritual, ethical or vocational.

Islam also has a holistic view of learning. It considers it impossible to separate the mundane, empirical and spiritual aspects of man and his education. Contemporary education is often devoid of the spiritual dimension and bereft of moral teachings necessary to lead a healthy life. Islamic education seeks to correct that imbalance and fashion the student's understanding of his world on the firm belief in a purposeful creation. It also insists that knowledge has to give rise to practice. Islamic education must therefore encompass all that is necessary to make education meaningful in daily life and propel the student towards the actualisation of what is learnt.

Educational Administration

The central administration of Syedna based in Mumbai, recognised as Dawat-e-Hadiyah, has three departments that oversee the implementation of his educational programme. The first is 'Al-Jamea-tus-Saifiyah', which runs the administration of the academy in Surat and Karachi and organises the dissemination of education to the community at large. The second is 'Daeratut Tarbiyat wa Attalim', which looks after the hundreds of *madrasa*s and schools all over the world, allocates teachers and runs a teacher-training institute in India. The third is the department of 'Al-Madrasa-tus-Saifiya-tul-Burhaniyah', which runs special primary and secondary schools in India, Pakistan. UAE and East Africa.

Islamic English

Syedna has also supported the movement towards the establishment of Islamic English. English is the world's international language, but its contemporary use is not conducive to expressing Islamic norms and values and Qur'anic concepts. Translation often falls short of conveying meaning and the cultural and utilitarian elements of the English language make it unsuitable for articulating Islam. The word mosque, for example, though derived from the original Arabic *masjid* and despite being redolent with Eastern mysticism, fails to convey the meaning of the original as a place of prostration (*sajda*). Muslim scholars have proposed the incorporation of Islamic terms into English to redress the situation and words such as *imam*, *hajj* and *halal* have already been integrated into the language.

A large number of primary and secondary schools serve the Bohra community all over India, with at least one in almost every city with a sizeable Bohra population. The Saifi High School in Mumbai for example, is well known particularly for the rounded education it provides young men, building academic skills together with vocational abilities.

The Burhani College of Commerce and Arts in Mumbai, founded in 1970 works in three shifts through the day, making higher education accessible to working students who would otherwise find it impossible to pursue higher studies. It is known for its moral discipline and standards.

Activities in
Al-Madrasa-tus-
Saifiya-tul-Burhaniyah
in Mumbai, India.

Though hundreds of schools run all over the world under Syedna's auspices, he has given particular attention to those that encourage a natural development of the early home-based upbringing of the child. These schools, called Al-Madrasa-tus-Saifiya-tul-Burhaniyah are in effect pioneering an Islamicised educational curriculum for primary and secondary education. There are eighteen such *madrasa*s operating in India, Pakistan, UAE, Kenya, Tanzania and Madagascar. When inaugurating the *madrasa* in Nairobi, Kenya, Syedna said that the *madrasa* represented the commencement of an educational revival.

Sports Centre of Al-Madrasa-tus-Saifiya-tul-Burhaniyah, Nairobi, Kenya.

Al-Madrasa-tus-Saifiya-tul-Burhaniyah, Karachi, Pakistan.

Restored 12th century Fatimi
motif. Al-Aqmar, Cairo.

REVIVAL
OF FATIMI
ARCHITECTURE

'He only shall tend Allah's masjids who believes in Allah and the Last Day
and establishes prayer and pays zakāh and fears none but Allah. For such
is it possible to be rightly guided.'

AL-QUR'AN 9:18

'We have endeavoured to blend Islamic values and architectural features from
various periods of Islamic history into these buildings and structures. Fatimi
monuments stand distinguished by their unique beauty. We have tried to express
our beliefs and ideologies through these buildings till they speak out in the
tongue of brick, stone and mortar and find expression in their arches, miḥrābs and
minarets. As long as belief is steadfast in the heart, it is not possible for it to be
precluded from expression.'

SYEDNA MOHAMMED BURHANUDDIN

REVIVAL OF FATIMI ARCHITECTURE

ARCHITECTURE, like any art, is an expression of a philosophy of life and a continuity of culture. If the architecture is religious in purpose, it represents the vitality of religious values that a people hold dear in life and a synthesis of those values for the ultimate purpose of life. Being an expression of the interpretation of Islam by the Fatimi *imāms*, Fatimi architecture animates the history, faith and beliefs of the Dawoodi Bohras and the contemporary revival of Fatimi architecture is seen as an assertion of that faith.

To initiate such a revival, Syedna Mohammed Burhanuddin ﷺ began the landmark restoration of Cairo's thousand year old al-Jāmi' al-Anwar, one of the world's largest *masjid*s. Completed in 1400/1980, it was a courageous task undertaken at great cost and risk and requiring strenuous research. The aim of the restoration was not simply a preservation of a historical monument for academic study, which often reduces the restored monument to a museum piece, but a reinstatement of the monument to the purpose for which it was built. This restoration was to have a momentous impact on the community, who for the first time participated in an international project and rescued a sacred monument that lay ruined. Since then, Syedna has restored three other Fatimi *masjid*s in Cairo. The restorations have fostered a renewed interest in Fatimi architecture, a fresh study of Fatimi architectural and design principles, and the manner in which these features infuse sacredness to the structure to which they are applied.

Deriving benefit from these restorations, Syedna Mohammed Burhanuddin ﷺ has fostered an era of unprecedented growth of building works, from *masjid*s and mausolea to schools and rest homes. He has encouraged the use of Fatimi architectural principles in such works, to articulate the community's values and reclaim its heritage.

The community has seen itself build *masjid*-complexes almost everywhere in the world where Bohras reside, that is, the Asian subcontinent, Middle East, Far East, Africa, Europe and North America. Fatimi characteristics and qualities have been imbibed in every new structure built and, in this way, a meaningful revival of Fatimi architecture has been effected. Along with the contemporary application of thousand year old styles, evident in their design, is the Islamic idea of creating infrastructures that combine the *masjid* (mosque), the *madrasa* (school), the home and the society to reflect and express all the elements of one's personal lifestyle as an integrated whole. Therefore such building works have had a concordant effect on the strengthening of the identity and culture of the Dawoodi Bohras.

Cairo, or more accurately, Al-Mu'izziya al-Qāhira, founded by the 14th *imām*, al-Moiz li-Dinillah, in the 10th century, is also known as the city of a thousand minarets. Amongst its largest monuments is al-Jāmi' al-Anwar, one of the world's largest *masjid*s. Exposed to the vagaries of time, the sacred structure had virtually been reduced to rubble. It was used as a military camp by the French and British, and later as a storage depot and a school's playground. In the 1970s, al-Anwar had been included by UNESCO in its plan to restore historical buildings in Old Cairo, but deterred by the magnitude of the project, it dropped the masjid from its restoration undertaking. Syedna took over the project and restored al-Jāmi' al-Anwar at his own cost, as an act of love and dedication to the 16th *imām*, al-Hakim bi-Amrillah, who had built it in the 4th/10th century. A house of Allah was restored to its original purpose and an oasis of cleanliness and spirituality established in an area of neglect.

During the excavation, two fragments of a tablet proclaiming the building of the al-Anwar ten centuries ago were discovered. One of these fragments bore sections of the name of the *imām*. Six other fragments existed in the Cairo Museum. These were used to reconstruct the tablet by referring to a drawing of the tablet by a British official stationed in Cairo in 1860 CE that was preserved in an arts magazine. The tablet was found to proclaim Imām al-Hakim bi-Amrillah, as the builder of the *masjid* the construction of which was resumed in 393 (1003CE). The attributes before the name of the *imām* are "the servant of Allah and His intimate".

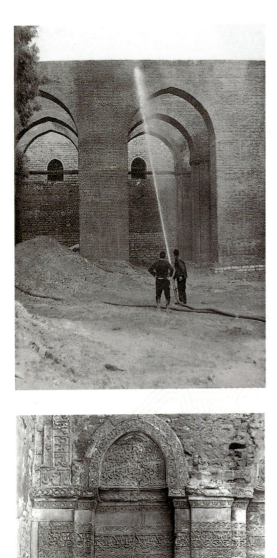

The restoration of al-Anwar, completed in 1980, took 27 months. Each facet of the restoration and repair was meticulously supervised by Syedna personally. Extensive research was carried out by a team of experts, including the renowned architect, Hasan Fathy. The dedication of the community to the project was inspiring. Men and women of all ages turned up from different parts of the world to contribute in whatever way they could to undertake this work of devotion. Many sat for hours reciting the Qur'an, invoking spiritual blessings for the endeavour. As the richness of Fatimi design and its architectural values were reassembled, it was as if a process of self-discovery had been initiated.

During the initial excavation, a centuries-old well was uncovered within the precincts of al-Anwar, and brought to life. Its waters became invaluable in the restoration work and today those who drink from it talk of its curative properties.

A Recollection

'Being six years old, it was difficult to grasp the actual size and nobility of the *masjid* that I stood in that magical day in 1980. Only a few hours earlier, my father had described it to me on the plane from California. Having lived in the West where such historical Islamic structures did not exist, I had yearned to see this newly renovated *masjid* that represented so much of my history.

Now that I was in it, I was held in a state of utter amazement as the majestic structure swallowed me. Its immense size spanned the blue horizon with ease. Its overall simplicity contrasted starkly with the details of individual shapes of fabrication. I had never been so overwhelmed. In a distance, I saw our leader, Syedna Mohammed Burhanuddin walking with grace and a pleasant countenance, glancing at parts of al-Anwar, inspecting the details of the well in the middle of it, and gazing at the towering minarets. He noticed with pleasure, people like me who had come from different parts of the world, applying the finishing touches and preparing the building for the opening ceremony the next day.

As I saw my mother pick up a broom and start sweeping, I found one myself and joined her. What better way to express my love and devotion to the sacred edifice than to lose myself in doing the most menial of services to it.'

A 26 YEAR OLD STUDENT OF ARABIC RESIDING IN USA

A short distance from al-Anwar is al-Aqmar, built by the 20th *imām*, al-Amir bi-Ahkamillah, in 519/1125. It was the next Fatimi structure to be restored, the work drawing to completion in 1996. Though much smaller than al-Anwar, many of its original features have survived weathering and neglect. A treasury of conception and design, the portal of al-Aqmar is among the most complex in Islamic architecture. The portal itself introduces the Verse of Light from the Qur'an which is then used as a theme throughout the structure in its ornamentation. Above its entrance is a typical Fatimi keel-arch with niche ribbing and a verse-medallion set in its centre. Al-Aqmar has often been cited for its importance in being one of the first *masjid*s to be incorporated within the urban design of the city by having its external facade aligned to the street whilst using wall thickness to align its interior with the direction of Makkah.

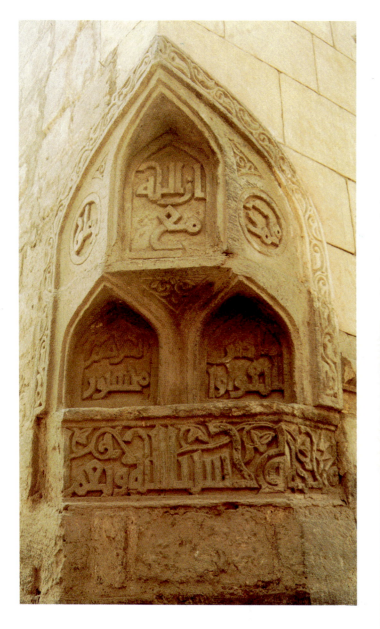

A unique feature of al-Aqmar is its *muqarnas* in each of the two corners of the front wall that interweave a verse from the Qur'an with the names Mohammed and Ali. This *muqarnas* has been used in several recent constructions, embellishing the new structures with one of the finest manifestations of Fatimi art.

Another treasure of Fatimi design preserved in Al-Aqmar is the *Shubbak al-Mishkāt*, a symbolic engraving depicting a lamp of enlightenment under the inscription of the affirmation of the oneness of Allah and the names of the Prophet and his successor. A lamp based on the original shape was fabricated and hundreds of them were used to light up the restored al-Anwar. The lamp, thus known as *Mishkāt al-Anwar* embellishes numerous other Fatimi monuments in Cairo as well as the *miḥrāb*s in many *masjid*s all over the world.

Replicated design in al-Masjid al-Fatimi, Karachi, Pakistan.

Restored design inside al-Aqmar illumined by a lamp replicated from the design itself.

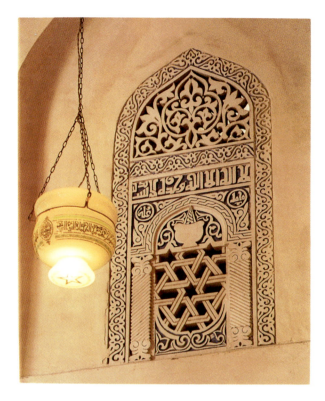

One of the first acts of al-Qaid Jawhar, the commander-in-chief of Imām al-Moiz, on conquering Egypt was to build a *masjid* as part of the founding of the city of Cairo. This *masjid,* al-Jāmi' al-Azhar, built on detailed personal instructions of Imām al-Moiz, was completed in 361/972. Al-Azhar not only defined the architecture favoured by the *imāms,* but also established the centre of a new city. Later, in 378/989, it became a university, the first in the world, and served the Fatimi empire as its centre of learning. The architecture of al-Azhar has been added to by successive rulers of Egypt, but its essentially Fatimi character remains to this day. Al-Azhar has also continued to remain the foremost institution of learning in the Islamic world through the centuries since it was first built. The original *miḥrāb* of Imām al-Moiz still exists in al-Azhar and has recently been renovated and symbolically embellished with *Mishkāt al-Anwar.*

Al-Lu'lu'a, a place where the 16th *imām*, al-Hakim bi-Amrillah, retired during the night for supplication, was so ruined that few of its original features were recognisable. Using elements from the other monuments of the period, al-Lu'lu'a has been magnificently restored. One of its unique features is the existence of a *miḥrāb* on each of its 3 floors.

Fatimi Architecture

The Fatimi *imāms*, descendants of Fatima ☘, the daughter of the Prophet Mohammed al-Mustafa ☙, ruled over much of the Islamic world from their capital in Cairo in the 10th, 11th and 12th centuries. They were great patrons of the arts and developed a unique architectural style that influenced the Islamic and European worlds for centuries. This architectural style, known as Fatimi, used Islamic themes to define an enclosed space and evolved a decorative character that uniquely blended simplicity and humility with Islamic spirituality. One of its contributions to design was its amalgamation of the derivations of the square into Kufi calligraphy and the use of floriation within it. Unfortunately, very few Fatimi monuments survived the vicissitudes of time and history. Those that are left exist mainly in Egypt, in the form of a few precious *masjids* and the monumental gates of Old Cairo.

The elements of Fatimi architecture are still a subject of research. One can say that the architecture is strongly focused on expressing the esoteric theology that forms part of the Fatimi interpretations of Islam. The use of light, for example, as a symbol of salvational knowledge emanating from the Qur'an, is commonly used both in the structure and the embellishment. Fatimi designs generally avoid profusion and tend to be austere, clean and firm. Ornamentation is restricted to carvings in stone, natural materials and stucco, working on principles of plane, shadow and light, resulting in elegance and sobriety rather than ostentation. Their use of geometrical borders and dados is also generally restrained. Layering consists of both, a layering of planes and patterns. Thus, even within the Islamic tradition of architecture, the Fatimi style strikes one as particularly modern.

The corner *muqarnas* called *Rukn al-Mukhallaq* (the perfumed corner) of al-Aqmar depicts typically Fatimi features. Its practicality in embellishing a complex corner is overshadowed by the spiritual significance of its honeycombed arches that, according to one interpretation, form the shape of a heart pointing heaven-wards. Its theological significance is underscored by the Qur'anic verse within it "Allah is with the pious and the benevolent" which speaks of dual desirable qualities in man. The names of the Prophet and his successor, Ali, embellish its two sides. Each name is placed to the side of the word *"ma'a"*, formed of the two letters *mīm* and *'ayn*, which are the initiating letters of the two names as well as part of the Qur'anic verse. In that way, the word placed centrally in the *muqarnas* plays a dual role. The unification of these themes of dual meanings within the design of the *muqarnas* is nothing short of genius. The design also has the other distinction of being one of the few surviving ones to bear the names of the Prophet and Ali together, and having been discovered, has been carefully used in selected new constructions of the community.

Badr al-Jamali, the Commander-in-Chief of the 18th *imām*, al-Mustansir billah, built Jāmiʿ al-Juyūshī at the top of a strategic peak in Cairo called Jabal al-Muqaṭṭam. This structure, also rich in Fatimi embellishment was restored in 1996.

The restored *miḥrāb* of al-Juyūshī.

The *miḥrāb* of al-Juyūshī has
inspired the one in al-Masjid
al-Fatimi in Raudat Tahera
complex, Mumbai, India (LEFT)
and was recently fully
replicated in al-Masjid al-
Muazzam, Surat, India (ABOVE).

The 8th, 9th and 10th *imāms* lived a life of seclusion in Salamiya, Syria in the 9th century CE. From there, they continued to guide the faithful through their functionaries spread all over the Islamic world. A *masjid* built by Imām Abdullah al-Radi, the 8th *imām*, near his residence lay derelict and unused until Syedna restored it in 1994.

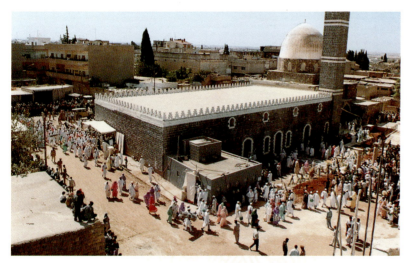

In Hus, Yemen, the *masjid* of the 1st *dāʿī*, Syedna Zoeb ibn Musa al-Wadii has been rebuilt on the basic structural plan of Fatimi architecture in Egypt and has also had its complex *miḥrāb* restored to original detail.

A particularly interesting renovation is that of al-Masjid al-Muazzam, in Surat, India, first built in 1219/1804 by the 43rd *dāʿī*, Syedna AbdeAli Saifuddin. The renovated *masjid* has profusely used Fatimi designs and is replete with a Fatimi ambience, yet elements of its Indian origin have been maintained. Completed in 1997, with an activity attracting thousands of Bohras eager to add their labour of love to its construction, it is the largest in the Bohra world.

Al-Masjid al-Hatimi in Zahra in the mountain range of Haraz, Yemen, rebuilt in 1995.

As the Dawoodi Bohras spread over the world, they sought to build *masjid*s and community complexes to cater for their spiritual and socio-cultural needs. These buildings have benefited from the rediscovered Fatimi architectural tradition yet blend in with local architectural landscape. The opening of these *masjid*s is attended by thousands in the moving ceremony of the dedication (*waqf*) of the house of worship to Allah.

Al-Masjid al-Husaini, London, completed in 1997, is within a large complex that includes 22 houses. Its confident portal was inspired by a Fatimi monument in Mahdiyya, Tunisia. His Royal Highness, Prince Charles visited the *masjid* under construction in 1996 and remarked, "Your commitment to building this very special place of worship of such beauty, I think, is of great credit to your community."

Al-Masjid al-Burhānī, Kalang, Malaysia, built in 1997.

Al-Masjid al-Sayfī, Toronto, Canada. Completed in 1990, it was one of the first *masjid*s built by the Bohras in the West.

Al-Masjid al-Sayfī in Dallas, Texas, opened in 1998. Its architecture has won it the 1999 Texas Society of Architects Design Award.

Al-Masjid al-Mohammedi, Houston, Texas, built in 1996.

Al-Masjid al-Burhānī, Nairobi, Kenya is part of a complex, which contains a school, sports facilities and housing block of 81 flats and houses. It was inaugurated in 1998.

Al-Masjid al-Quṭbī, Coimbatore, India, opened in 1997.

The largest of five *masjid*s, al-Masjid al-Burhānī in the famous old town, Mombasa, Kenya, was rebuilt in 1993. It is located amidst a historical setting with strong Islamic and Portuguese influences yet its own architecture stands out in the old harbour.

Al-Masjid al-Sayfī, Reunion (BELOW) and al-Masjid al-Burhānī, Fort Dauphin, Madagascar (RIGHT), both opened in 1999, along with al-Masjid al-Ḥakīmī, in Mayotte, are the first *masjid*s built by Bohras in the French-speaking world.

Al-Masjid al-Sayfī, Dubai, inaugurated in 1983.

Syedna Mohammed Burhanuddin succeeded to the office of al-Dai al-Mutlaq in 1965. Since then, to date, 140 new *masjid*s have been built by the community, and a further 90 are planned or under construction. These are spread in 20 countries in the Indian subcontinent, the Far East, the Middle East, East Africa, Europe and North America. Most of the constructions have taken place after the renovation of al-Jāmi' al-Anwar in 1980 from which all subsequent building works have drawn inspiration and after which Fatimi design became more readily available to the community's architectural repertoire. The building of these houses of worship has transformed the Bohra community and given a focus to their spiritual endeavours.

Raudat Tahera, the mausoleum of Syedna Taher Saifuddin, the predecessor, father and mentor of the present Syedna is a testimony to his greatness. Built over a period of 11 years and completed in 1976, it is an architectural marvel, displaying a rare balance of simplicity and grandeur. It was the first mausoleum in India to lavishly imbibe Fatimi design principles, heralding a new age in building activity. Located in the heart of Bhindi Bazaar in Mumbai, where the Bohras live in concentration, it is an oasis of bliss and relief for the thousands of pilgrims who throng there recalling the memory of their spiritual father who led them so benignly for over 50 years. The Raudat Tahera complex houses three of the main manifestations of Islamic architecture in an exquisite *masjid*, the mausoleum itself, and a symbolic garden.

Raudat Tahera

The sheer mass of Raudat Tahera, and its huge dome lend it a commanding presence. Yet, despite its simple and symmetrical geometry, the mausoleum possesses an elegance that immediately arrests the observer as if emanating a spiritual aura that touches the soul. The apparent asceticism of the exterior of Raudat Tahera belies its internal complexity, for within it, the walls are but pages of the Qur'an written in gold. The Qur'an looks down upon a solitary grave that lies humbly in the middle. This sight evokes a rare sense of spirituality that captivates the pilgrim. The vast interior space stretches from a square base, depicting the principle of earth, to a spherical dome suggesting the crowning firmament to which man is to ascend. The glow of the Qur'an on the walls creates a unique aura of resplendent yet austere spirituality. The dimensions of the structure represent facets of the life of Syedna Taher Saifuddin and his scholarship and devotion to the *imāms* are depicted in the selections of his prose and poetry written on the walls under the Qur'an.

The Raudat Tahera captures the persona of Syedna Taher Saifuddin, which like the internal majesty of Raudat Tahera, was a never-ending source of knowledge and spirituality and an epitome of the highest ideals of Islamic intellectualism.

Although much of the design of the mausoleum is Fatimi in origin, its architectural detail has a touch of Indian elements. This contrast provides a visually pleasing blend of strength and intricacy. The Qur'an inscribed in its entirety in its interior makes it the only monument in the world to attempt such a calligraphic accomplishment. All the verses are laid with gold leaf, some of them bejewelled to adorn the words of revelation. These embellishments, though rich, impart a unique atmosphere of serenity and spirituality to the tomb. The inscriptions have been replicated from a hand-written manuscript of the Qur'an used by Syedna Taher Saifuddin during his lifetime. Each page was carefully separated, replicated on marble and the original Qur'an rebound.

In 1965, the mausoleum of the 17th century martyr, Syedna Qutbuddin Shahid, the 32nd *dāʿī*, was opened in Ahmedabad, India. An ambitious structure in the Mughal style constructed during the time of Syedna Taher Saifuddin, it is now one of the architectural landmarks of Ahmedabad and a place of pilgrimage for Bohras from all over the world. Ahmedabad was one of the early seats of the *dāʿī*s in India in the 16th century CE. In the 15th and 16th centuries, Dawoodi Bohras often fell victim to intolerant rulers and thousands were slain. These martyrs are buried around this mausoleum in an area known as the Mazar-e-Qutbi.

In 1996, four other mausolea of *dāʿī*s within the Mazar-e-Qutbi were rebuilt. Each mausoleum was required to be unique yet blend aesthetically with the main mausoleum of the complex. Each had to continue to articulate the qualities of its original architecture, and yet be infused with the freshness of Fatimi features. The mausolea, successfully completed, now form masterpieces of delicate blends. They cover the graves of four *dāʿī*s of the 16th and 17th centuries.

FACING PAGE, CLOCKWISE FROM TOP LEFT
The mausolea of Syedna Dawood ibn Ajabshah Burhanuddin (26th *dāʿī*), Syedna Dawood ibn Qutubshah Burhanuddin (27th *dāʿī*), from whom the Dawoodi Bohras derive their name, Syedna Shaykh Adam Safiyuddin (28th *dāʿī*) and Syedna AbdulTayyib Zakiyuddin (29th *dāʿī*).

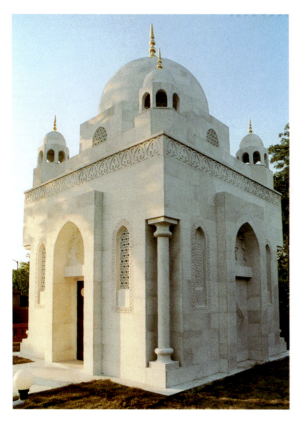

Qubbah Badriyyah in Jamnagar, India, the mausoleum of the 34th *dāʿī*, Syedna Ismail Badruddin was completed in 1993. One of its unique features is its finely-crafted marble doorway in filigree, that allows a natural air-flow within the mausoleum. It has maintained many of its pre-renovation Mughal and local architectural features.

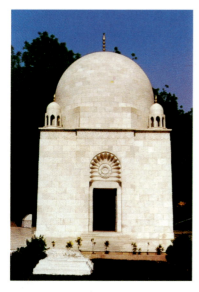

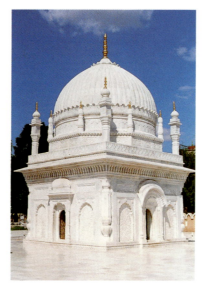

The mausoleum of the 25th *dāʿī*, Syedna Jalal Shamsuddin built in Mazar-e-Qutbi in Ahmedabad in 1981 draws its architectural inspiration from the Raudat Tahera, though its doorway is a replica of the ribbed niche of the portal of al-Aqmar, Cairo.

The mausoleum of Syedi Abdul Qadir Hakimuddin, the renowned scholar and poet, in Burhanpur, India, was rebuilt in 1996, maintaining all its 18th century features.

The mausoleum of Bawa Mulla Khan in Rampura, India, was built in 1986.

The mausoleum of Malik al-Ashtar, the loyal companion of Ali ibn Abi Talib who was poisoned on his way to Egypt where he was to act as governor. This burial site in a suburb of Cairo, Egypt, was first visited by Syedna with his predecessor in 1356/1937. Situated in a remote and peaceful farm, the grave was in a simple room until Syedna built the tomb of the great martyr in 1998.

The mausoleum of Syedna Hatim Muhyiddin, the 3rd *dā'ī*, in al-Hutayb. Along with the mausoleum, Syedna also built a road to it in 1976 to ease the difficult journey undertaken by pilgrims for 800 years. This road has been recently widened and tarmacked. Three *masjid*s on the mountain have also been restored.

The mausoleum and *masjid* of the 37th *dā'ī*, Syedna Nur Mohammed Nuruddin in Kutch Mandvi were rebuilt in 1999. Minarets and door archways of the old mausoleum have not been discarded but have been reused in *masjid*s in India and USA.

All the mausolea built by Syedna have been designed with similar briefs. There was always an attempt to combine the relevant period style with the Fatimi heritage. Visited by hundreds of pilgrims each day, their functional practicality was always to be kept in mind. Embellishments were not to be lavish but had to express the revered persons' spirituality and enhance the tombs' tranquillity and sacredness.

12th century floral Fatimi
motif, Al-Aqmar, Cairo.

A NOBLE
UPBRINGING

'O my son, establish prayer, enjoin what is good and forbid
what is evil; and bear with patience what befalls you. These are
indeed acts of courage and resolve.'

AL-QUR'AN 31:17

'I have endeavoured to give him a noble upbringing,
a fine instruction and a refinement in culture,
and now he is a man of wisdom and
accomplished learning.'

SYEDNA TAHER SAIFUDDIN ﷺ IN PRAISE OF
HIS SON AND SUCCESSOR.

A NOBLE UPBRINGING

NOWHERE has the continuity of a legacy been more starkly visible than in the way tradition was handed down from father to son, from mentor to disciple, from accomplished scholar to ardent student, as it has been from Syedna Taher Saifuddin ṣ to Syedna Mohammed Burhanuddin ṣ. The transmission of religious values and a religious heritage entailed not only the thorough imbibing of theological texts but a process of spiritual refinement that was from its very inception personally supervised by a meticulous father.

Syedna was born the first son to Syedna Taher Saifuddin ṣ on the day of celebration of his accession to the august office of al-Dai al-Mutlaq on 20th Rabī' al-Ākhar 1333, corresponding to 6th March 1915. Knowing that his son was to succeed him in an era of turbulent changes, when the world would move from the problems of industrialisation and rapid economic growth into the cultural and paradigmatic complexities of the post-modern era, Syedna Taher Saifuddin ṣ trained and groomed him for that eventuality. He prepared his heir-apparent personally and kept him by his side through his rigorous schedule of daily activities to make his every gesture and every act an experience of education.

At an early age, Syedna Mohammed Burhanuddin ṣ had committed the Qur'an to memory and acquired the maturity of the learned. At 19, he was raised to the position of *ma'ẓūn*, the highest position under the *dā'ī* and was designated successor to the office of al-Dai al-Mutlaq. That the successor to the august office was known for three decades, enabled the community to benefit from the heir-apparent throughout the period.

In the process, an age-old legacy based on the careful preservation and assimilation of religious values was handed down from one who had led the community in an era of momentous world events spanning the whole of the first half of the 20th century to one who would carry the burden of that leadership into the 21st.

Thus, with the demise of Syedna Taher Saifuddin ṣ, despite having lost an exalted leadership that had steered it successfully through a difficult period of internal dissent compounded with external social upheavals, a seamless transition occurred with Syedna Mohammed Burhanuddin ṣ that allowed the community to consolidate the achievements of the past years into the fruitfulness that one sees in the best periods of prosperity.

Syedna Taher Saifuddin personally undertook the training of his son and spared no effort to ensure that the task was thoroughly executed. He said of his son, "I started his education with the name of Allah, endowing him with the best in our culture, taught him good manners and enriched him with Islamic philosophy, chapter by chapter, book after book. He has striven with me to reach the position I intended to take him, to the final phase of the treasures of knowledge reposed in us by the Fatimi *imām*s. All this I did while the demands on my time were heavy, facing onslaughts to the *da'wah*. I am happy that I have now brought him to this stage, when by Allah's grace, he will become like me."

The *mīṣāq* (oath) is the most important rite of passage in the faith of the Dawoodi Bohras. The initiate submits himself to the representative of Allah to pledge his entry into the fold by making a covenant with Allah. This is strengthened by an oath of allegiance to the *imām* of the time and the *imām*'s *dā'ī*. Seen here is the official portrait of Syedna Mohammed Burhanuddin after having made this commitment to his father and *dā'ī* in 1349/1930.

Even as a child, Syedna travelled with his father and accompanied him for *ziyārat* (pilgrimage) and other journeys throughout the world. He performed *ḥajj* for the first time at the age of 15, immediately after his *mīṣāq*. This early preparation was portentious of the gruelling amount of travel that Syedna's schedule requires of him even at his advanced age. Seen above is Syedna with his predecessor in pilgrimage at Jerusalem in the year 1356/1937 at the age of 24.

During the seclusion of the *imām*, the *dāʿī* heads the *daʿwah* as the *imām*'s representative and vicegerent and occupies the paramount position of authority. Two other *rutba*s (ranks of religious hierarchy) of the *daʿwah*, the *maʾzūn* and the *mukāsir* also exist as subordinates to the *dāʿī*. The occupants of these *rutba*s are appointed by the *dāʿī*. Syedna Taher Saifuddin appointed his son, Syedna Mohammed Burhanuddin as *maʾzūn* and also designated him to be his heir-apparent (*manṣūṣ*) in the year 1352/1933. Seen above is an official portrait of Syedna, at the age of 19, soon after the designation.

When the *imām* chose seclusion in 526/1132, the *dāʿīs* administered the *imām's daʿwah* from Yemen. For over four centuries, they preserved the faith and sustained the fold from their bases in Yemen, but then, in 946/1539, the seat of the *daʿwah* was transferred to India from where the *dāʿīs* continue to function to this day. Difficult circumstances and geographical logistics prevented the *dāʿīs* of India from re-visiting this blessed land of their predecessors, until in 1382/1961, Syedna Mohammed Burhanuddin was sent to Yemen to assess the condition of the faithful there, to re-establish their links with the *daʿwah* and to research the burial places of the great *dāʿīs* of Yemen. He returned having won the hearts of the Yemeni community and having performed the *ziyārat* of his predecessors. Even the prevalent political hostility changed to hospitality. So successful was his visit that Syedna Taher Saifuddin bestowed upon him the historically significant title of *"Manṣūr al-Yaman"* (BELOW). The significance of this title is enormous. The only other person known by this epiteth has been the great *dāʿī* Abul Qasim, in the 3rd/9th century. The veracity of the bestowal, meaning "One aided to victory (by Allah) in Yemen", was appreciated further when in a courageous act in 1391/1971, he mitigated discordant elements, saved the Yemeni community from alienation and dramatically changed its fortunes. Today the community of the region is spiritually and materially prosperous and strongly devoted to its faith and heritage.

Syedna Mohammed Burhanuddin's closeness to and personal rapport with his predecessor allowed him to observe his functioning in the day-to-day affairs of the *da'wah* – a unique training environment to a future successor. At all hours, through personal attention or the delegation of duties, Syedna was tutored with thoroughness. Syedna Taher Saifuddin was always pleased with his qualities and once wrote "Mohammed is praised by everyone and the mere mention of his name is sufficient to evoke the image of his eminence."

Rarely has the training of the successor been so complete and the inheritance of a heritage so comprehensive. This is best depicted by an event that took place in Ahmedabad in 1373/1953 unique in the history of the *wa'ẓ* tradition of the *da'wah*. The father and son, predecessor and successor sat together on the *takht* (sermon seat) and the successor picked up the thread of discourse with complete mastery to the contentment of his mentor.

Syedna's imbibing of attributes necessary for the high office destined for him, and his knowledge and erudition elated the heart of his predecessor, who frequently praised his son's abilities and conferred upon him the unique titles, *Tāj al-Da'wah al-Ṭayyibiyya al-Gharrā'*, *Qurrat 'ayn Imām al-Muttaqīn* and *'Umdat al-'Ulamā al-Muwaḥḥidīn*. Roughly translated into English, they mean, "Crown of the radiant *Da'wah Ṭayyibiyya*", "Dearest to the *imām* of the pious" and "Doyen of the learned affirmers of Unity (of Allah)". These are encapsulated as a calligraphic crown (ABOVE) made in the year of his ascension to office. In addition, he was conferred the degree of *al-'Alīm al-Rāsikh*, being the highest attainment of learning.

This photograph graphically depicts the handing over of traditions. The harmony and correspondence of mentor and disciple is striking in their attire and mannerism. Syedna Taher Saifuddin was so contented with his son's preparation for office that he said of him in a poem: "This young man is none other than I. He is a noble repository of the knowledge of guidance."

No other event in contemporary Bohra history shook the community as did the demise of Syedna Taher Saifuddin in 1385/1965. Having been at the helm of the community for half a century and seen it through tumultuous periods, his loss was nothing short of calamitous. It was in this moment that his successor, Syedna Mohammed Burhanuddin, became the source of solace and strength to the grief-torn thousands, though his own loss was greater. Seen here are grieving followers offering condolences and being themselves consoled, and the offering of *mīṣāq* to the new incumbent to the office of al-Dai al-Mutlaq.

Syedna's scholarship and erudition were soon recognised by al-Azhar and Aligarh universities as Syedna took office. Both honoured educational establishments, one representing a tradition stretching back 10 centuries to the Fatimi Imāms and the other, established about 150 years ago to cater for the aspirations of the modern Muslims, conferred doctorates on Syedna.

بسم الله الرحمن الرحيم

الجمهورية العربية المتحدة

جَامِعَةُ الأزْهَر

The honorary Doctorate of Islamic Sciences was conferred on Syedna by al-Azhar University, Cairo, at the recommendation of President Gamal Abdel Nasser, on 21st Zilqa'da 1385, corresponding to 13th March 1966. Part of the citation reads "If the son is true to his father as experiences testify, then the leader, the sultan Mohammed Burhanuddin has broadness of vision, interest in learning and knowledge, sincerity in Allah and aspires to forge bonds between Islamic sects. These qualities make the hope in him firmer, increase the good expected of him and make surer the anticipation that he will be a worthy successor to a good predecessor, *Inshā' Allah*. The late sultan (Syedna Taher Saifuddin) stood for a rational call for closeness of Islamic sects despite their differences in their schools of *fiqh*. It was his desire that men of learning should shun pettiness and attend to dispelling doubts cast against Islam by its enemies. With this generous spirit and good hope, I announce the presidential decree by which he has granted the degree of doctorate honoris causa, from the University of al-Azhar to al-Sayyid, al-Ustāz, al-'Allāma Mohammed Burhanuddin, leader of the Bohra Muslim Community."

Muslim University Gazette

Special Topics : Founder's Day
Special Convocation

Aligarh 8 November 1966   FORTNIGHTLY   Vol. 16 No. 5

The Citation

The following citation was read by the Vice-Chancellor at the Special Convocation.

Mr. Chancellor :

I seek your permission to present His Holiness Syedna Mohammed Burhanuddin Saheb, Head of the Dawoodi Bohra community, for conferment upon him of the Degree of Doctor of Theology Honoris Causa.

His Holiness belongs to an illustrious family, the custodians of the Fatimi tradition. That tradition stands for the highest moral and spiritual values in life and constitutes the basis of a society governed by high principles of conduct. A scion of the Fatimi Imams who founded Al-Azhar University at Cairo, the oldest University in the world, Syedna is himself the embodiment of learning and piety. In recognition of these great qualities, it was in the fitness of things that Al-Azhar University itself should have been the first to confer upon him, this very year, the Honorary Degree of Doctor of Islamic Science.

Besides being himself a scholar, His Holiness is a patron of learing who has been brought up in the traditions of his great father and has, therefore, both inherited and himself cultivated a broad and liberal humanism. This quality permeates the conduct of his high spiritual office, his bearing as a person and his relations with men. In requesting you to honour such a person, I seek due recognition of his eminence by this University, and I, therefore, pray that you be pleased to confer, on His Holiness the Degree of Doctor of Theology Honoris Causa.

Nawab Ali Yavar Jung, the Vice-Chancellor of Aligarh Muslim University, India, reading his citation which was later printed in the University Gazette. The honorary Doctorate of Theology was conferred on Syedna on 25th Rajab 1386, corresponding to 8th November 1966.

Syedna Taher Saifuddin, had received an honorary doctorate (of Theology) from Aligarh Muslim University in 1946, and later, in 1953, was elected to serve as chancellor. The appointment was made at a critical juncture when the partition of the Indian subcontinent had starved the university of its best minds. Syedna Taher Saifuddin had applied himself diligently to the needs and aspirations of the university and is warmly remembered by its former students to this day. His term in office was thrice renewed and he remained the chancellor of the university until his death in 1965. Seen here is Syedna Taher Saifuddin at the university with Prime Minister Jawaharlal Nehru and Dr. Zakir Husain, the then vice-chancellor and later President of India.

In August 1999, Aligarh Muslim University requested Syedna Mohammed Burhanuddin to take up its chancellorship. The vice-chancellor, Dr. M. Rahman, and other staff of the university visited Al-Jamea-tus-Saifiyah, Surat, in November 1999, to meet Syedna and to see at first hand, Syedna's own academic institution. Seen here, the party viewing the central room of Mahad al-Zahra, the Qur'an memorisation institute (LEFT) and the vice-chancellor joining in the oral exams of the academy. (RIGHT).

Syedna Mohammed Burhanuddin in the robe of chancellor of Aligarh Muslim University.

بسم الله الرحمن الرحيم ١٢ عام متسعة عيد الفطر
وبر و بو ليا استحسن ربيمو لي و تم با لخير بحق بمفح
يا حبيب العصر غياث ملاذ العبا د و يا شفيع العبد
يا نافع الولي يوم المعاد
الموءمن

يا حبيب العصر ملاذ العباد
و يا شفيع العبد يوم المعاد

يا مالك النفوس طو بي لمن
مصاحبة الدارين منك استفاد

An extract from Syedna's draft of a eulogy written for the *imām* on *'Īd al-fitr* 1412. The first line is an invocation of the name of Allah, the Compassionate, the Merciful, followed by the date of the poem. This is followed by an abbreviated supplication. The next lines are the composition of the first couplet, with alternatives clearly written out for consideration, followed by the author's choice for the final words.

Recently 857 such couplets of poetry, written specifically on the annual Muslim festival of *'Īd al-fitr* were published, from which these verses have been reproduced.

Al-Risāla al-Ramaḍāniyya

May Allah grace with ṣalawāt His messenger, through whom He put a seal to the final and most complete of His messages. And revealed unto him the Holy Qur'an in His act of revelation. And ordered him to recite it in recitation. And to remember and repeat the name of his Lord and to supplicate himself before Him in supplication. This messenger is indeed Mohammed ﷺ, the leader of the prophets and their crowning glory. And Allah says of him in the holy Qur'an, in testimony of his excellence over all prophets, and his exalted status, "It is indeed He who sent His messenger with guidance and the religion of truth that He may establish it above others". And granted him the distinction of proximity unto Him, and graced him with the brightest and noblest of favours. Elucidating this in the holy book, Allah says of him, "Then he drew near to Allah and closer still until he was no more than two bow arcs away and nearer still."

صلى الله عليه من نبي ختم به النبوة تتميا و تكميلا ٭
و نـزّل عليه القرآن تنزيلا ٭ وامره ان يرتله ترتيلا ٭
ويذ كراسم ربه ويتبتل اليه تبتيلا ٭ وفـضّله على
جميع الانبياء والمرسلين تفضيلا ٭ محمد سيد الرسل
الكرام ومن اتى لمفرقهم تاجا و اكليلا ٭ وقال في
ذكره الحكيم مظهرا لتفضيله على جميع رسله ومعبرا
عن عظيم محله ٭ « هو الذي ارسل رسوله بالهدى ودين
الحق ليظهره على الدين كله» ٭ واعطاه من رتبة الزلفى
عنده والكرامة لديه المحل الا سمى الا سنى ٭ موضحا
في كتابه الكريم ذلك المعنى ٭ بقوله سبحانه ۵ ثم دنى
فتد لى فكان قاب قوسين او ادنى »٭

An extract of a passage from Syedna's book of philosophical prose, written in his first year of incumbency to the office of al-Dai al-Mutlaq in 1966, based on an elaborative interpretation of the first chapter of the Qur'an ("The Opening"). Called *Istiftāḥ Zubadil Ma'ārif* (Initiation of the Essence of Knowledge) the book is written in a unique style extensively developed by his predecessor in 48 books of his own. It begins with an exquisitely composed supplication and eulogy followed by another section that blends a variety of topics and knowledge hierarchies into a continuous whole. Its style is remarkable both in its overall structure as well as in the fluidity of prose that allows references and allusions to be forcefully combined with new ideas. The quality of this particular passage lies in its traditional form of composition in which Qur'anic verses are incorporated seamlessly into the writer's expression of love for the Prophet. The delicate theological balance of Islamic veneration is perfectly handled with a mastery of Arabic language that lends a heightened eloquence to the emotion by rhythm.

Munājāt is a pleading to Allah, a supplication that is an intensely personal conversation with Allah. Syedna Mohammed Burhanuddin, following the tradition of his predecessor, composes a *munājāt* every year in the month of Ramaḍān, which is recited all over the world by his followers. The style is unique, consisting of classical Arabic poetry of tightly balanced verses suited to deep emotional expression. Extracts from his compositions *Al-munājāt al-raḍiyya al-salsaliyya* and *'Uyūn al-munājāt al-Ramaḍāniyya* written in 1403/1983 and 1404/1984 respectively show the poet in humble and intimate supplication before Allah. His choice and arrangement of words, often inspired by the Qu'ran and other traditional supplications, contribute to the lucidity of the poetry and express dimensions of spiritual meaning that lift the recitor to the heights of enlightened prayer.

Al-munājāt al-raḍiyya al-salsaliyya
1403/1983

أُنَاجِيكَ يَا رَبَّ الْبَرِيَّةِ لَاجِيَا   إِلَيْكَ وَلِلْغُفْرَانِ إِيَّاكَ رَاجِيَا

I plead with you, O Lord of Creation, as I seek refuge in you and bear hope of your pardon.

أُنَاجِيكَ يَا رَبِّي بِبَابِكَ وَاقِفًا   وَمِنْ عُظْمِ ذَنْبِي خَائِفًا رَبِّ رَاجِيَا

I plead with you, O my Lord, as I beckon at your door, fearing my sins so monumental.

وَأَدْعُوكَ لَيْلًا خَاشِعًا مُتَمَلْمِلًا   وَأَخْشَى ذُنُوبًا أَوْبَقَتْ وَمَعَاصِيَا

I supplicate in humility and lamentation in the dead of night, fearing those sins and lapses that lead to perdition.

فَتَرْعَشُ رِجْلِي ذَاكِرًا مَا اقْتَرَفْتُهُ   وَتُمْطِرُ آمَاقِي الدُّمُوعَ الْجَوَارِيَا

My legs give way and my eyes rain tears as I remember these sins of mine.

بِبَابِكَ عَبْدٌ مُذْنِبٌ جَاءَ ضَارِعًا   فَكُنْ رَاحِمًا آثَامَهُ رَبِّ عَافِيَا

At your door stands this sinful slave, grieving. Do have mercy on him and forgive his deficiencies.

ذُنُوبِي كَبِيرَاتٌ عُيُوبِي كَثِيرَةٌ   فَكُنْ غَافِرًا إِلِي كُلَّهَا رَبِّ مَاحِيَا

My sins are grave, my shortcomings many, forgive them, my Lord and expunge them all.

سِوَاكَ فَمَنْ اَرْجُوْ؟ لِذَنْبِي غَافِرًا وَغَيْرُكَ مَنْ اَدْعُوْ؟ لِكُرْبِي جَالِيَا

Who else may I seek forgiveness from? Who else shall I pray to lighten my burden?

اَنَا مُسْتَحِقُّ الْمَنْعِ لَوْ اَنْ مَنَعْتَنِي وَاِلَّا فَكُمْ قِدْمًا عَهِدْتُكَ حَابِيَا

If you deny me, I would be worthy of that; but I have known the surety of your bestowal.

مَوَدَّةَ قُرْبَى الْمُصْطَفَى مَنْ حَبَوْتَهُ اَتَجْعَلُهُ عَنْ بَابِ عَفْوِكَ قَاصِيَا

One on whom you have bestowed the love of kin of Muṣṭafā, would you distance from your pardon?

اَتَطْرُدُ؟ مِسْكِينًا يَؤُمُّ فِنَاءَهُمْ اِلَى بَيْتِ اَهْلِ الْبَيْتِ لِلْهَدْيِ اَوِيَا

Would you turn away a beggar who journies to the house of *Ahl al-Bayt* to seek refuge therein?

سِوَى وِرْدِهِمْ ذَا الْعَبْدُ وَاللهِ لَمْ يَرِدْ وَمِنْ غَيْرِ عِلْمِ الْحَقِّ لَمْ يَكُ رَاوِيَا

By Allah, this slave never drank but at the well of these *imāms*, never quenched his thirst
except with knowledge of righteousness.

لَكَ الْحَمْدُ حَمْدًا بَالِغًا اِذْ اَذِنْتَ لِي بِجَاهِهِمْ اَدْعُوْكَ رَبِّي مُنَادِيَا

I praise you abundantly that you allowed me to call for you and supplicate you, my Lord, through their high station.

لَكَ الشُّكْرُ شُكْرًا كَامِلًا اِذْ اَذِنْتَ لِلـ اُولَى فِيْهِمْ عَيَّنْتَنِي لَكَ دَاعِيَا

I thank you profusely that you gave me permission over those whom you made me *dāʿī*,

عَلَى مَنْهَلِ الْمَنْجَاةِ لِلْقَوْمِ رَائِدًا لِاُشْرِكَهُمْ فِيْ ذِي الْمُنَاجَاةِ دَاعِيَا

and over whose destiny (emancipation) you made me responsible for, to include in this pleading.

وَ"جَامِعَةٍ سَيْفِيَّةٍ" بِافْتِتَاحِهَا اَنِلْنِي فِيْ عِلْمِ الرَّشَادِ الْاَمَانِيَا

With the inauguration of Al-Jamea-tus-Saifiyah, fulfil my aspirations for knowledge of guidance.

لِاَفْتَحَ اَبْوَابَ الْمَعَارِفِ كُلَّهَا لِمَنْ كَانَ دُوْنَ الْقِشْرِ يَرْجُو الْمَعَانِيَا

So I may open the doors of enlightenment for those who seek the essence of meaning.

ʿUyūn al-munājāt al-Ramaḍāniyya
1404/1984

أُنَاجِيكَ يَا اَللهُ، يَارَبِّ، سَاجِدًا   وَأَدْعُوكَ يَامَوْلَايَ إِيَّاكَ عَابِدًا

I plead with you O Allah, O Lord, in prostration, and supplicate O my Master, immersed in worship.

أُنَاجِيكَ عَبْدًا خَاضِعًا عَارِبٍ خَاشِعًا   إِلَى بَابِكَ الْمَرْجُوِّ لِلْعَفْوِ وَافِدًا

I plead with you, a slave with humility and modesty, at your door of hope of forgiveness.

أُنَاجِيكَ عَبْدًا خَاشِيًا ذَنْبَهُ الَّذِي   تَعَاطَاهُ خَطَأً أَوْ تَعَاطَاهُ عَامِدًا

I plead with you, a slave in fear of his sins committed in error or with intent.

أُنَاجِيكَ رَبِّي لُؤْلُؤَ الدَّمْعِ نَاثِرًا   وَدُرَّ وَسِيلَاتِ الْمَكَارِمِ نَاضِدًا

I plead with you, my Lord, having shed pearls of tears and gathered pearls of intercession of your chosen ones.

أُنَاجِيكَ قَطْرَ الدَّمْعِ كَالْغَيْثِ مُسْبِلًا   وَمِنْ عِظَمِ خَوْفِ الذَّنْبِ كَالْغُصْنِ مَائِدًا

I plead with you, in a deluge of tears, wavering like a loose branch, in fear of my transgressions.

أَتَيْتُكَ أَثْقَالَ الذُّنُوبِ مُقَاسِيًا   وَجِئْتُكَ أَهْوَالَ الْخُطُوبِ مُكَابِدًا

I have come to you enduring the weight of my sins and bearing the dread of calamities.

أَتَيْتُ بِأَعْمَالٍ قِبَاحٍ رَدِيَّةٍ   إِلَى اللهِ أَشْكُو وِزْرَهَا الْمُتَصَاعِدًا

I have come to you with my abhorent and unworthy deeds, the burden of which is ever increasing.

قُمِ اللَّيْلَ مِنْكَ الْأَمْرُ مُمْتَثِلًا لَهُ   أَتَيْتُكَ لَيْلًا لِلْمُنَاجَاةِ سَاهِدَا

Heeding your call to observe the night vigil, I have come to plead to you in the dead of night.

وَكَيْفَ الَّذِي مِنْ مَوْتِهِ خَافَ بَغْتَةَ الْـ   بَيَاتِ حَثِيثًا غَفْلَةً نَامَ هَاجِدَا

How may one who fears the swiftness of death, sleep in stupor?

فَأَبْوَابُكَ اللّٰهُمَّ فِي اللَّيْلِ لَمْ تَزَلْ   مُفَتَّحَةً دَأْبًا لِمَنْ جَاءَ قَاصِدَا

For those who choose to journey to you, my Allah, your doors are always open.

خَزَائِنُكَ اللّٰهُمَّ مَا غُلِّقَتْ لَنَا   لِرَحْمَتِكَ الْأَسْبَابُ تُوْلِي الْفَوَائِدَا

Your treasures are never denied us, and the doors of your mercy are open to all.

فَبِالْإِذْنِ مِنْهُ كَمْ عَمَرْنَا الْمَسَاجِدَا   لِعِلْمِ هُدَاهُ كَمْ بَنَيْنَا الْمَعَاهِدَا

With his (*imām's*) sanction, we have raised many *masjids* and for his guiding
knowledge established many institutions.

عَمَارَتُنَا لِلْجَامِعِ الْأَنْوَرِ اغْتَدَتْ   عَوَائِدَ فَضْلٍ مِنْهُ جَلَّتْ عَوَائِدَا

We restored al-Jāmi' al-Anwar, through the grace and gift of the *imām*, a most precious gift.

أَرَى الْمُؤْمِنِينَ الْمُخْلِصِينَ وُجُوهُهُمْ   تُبَشِّرُ عَمَّا أَضْمَرُوهُ عَقَائِدَا

Sincere believers, I see their countenances give abundant expression to the faith in their hearts.

وَكُنْ لَهُمْ خَيْرَ الْمَكَاسِبِ زَائِدَا   وَكُنْ عَنْهُمْ شَرَّ الْمَعَاطِبِ ذَائِدَا

To them increase the boons of achievement and decrease the evil of ruin.

إِلٰهِي أَعِدْ مِنْ لَيْلَةِ الْقَدْرِ دَائِمًا   عَلَيْنَا جَمِيعًا خَيْرَهَا الْمُتَوَارِدَا

My Lord, make the continuous merits of Laylat al-Qadr return to us, always.

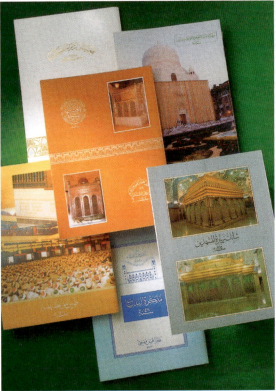

Syedna in his office, attending to files presented for his directions. It is said that no file remains in his office longer than twenty-four hours. His directions to the community and reports of his own activities are transmitted to the community through official communications called *miṣāl sharīf*. These documents provide a record of the era.

A Leader of Our Times

When one encounters Syedna Mohammed Burhanuddin, one has a sense of meeting a man resonating history in his appearance, demeanour, conduct and dignity. To understand him, one has to understand the tradition he carries and his acute awareness of this privilege and duty. He has always seen himself the servant of the *imām* and duty-bound to preserve and protect his followers, an injunction that he pursues with utter humility and complete devotion.

Syedna bids one to follow the *sharī'ah*, observe its ritual, adhere to its strictures and codes of conduct, respect the duties and responsibilities it lays down on one, and motivate oneself not by a need for ritual or religious discipline in one's life, but simply for the sake of Allah. He recognises that it cannot be fear of retribution, or need for material gain that could motivate the modern believer in an age where the economic system looks after what one uses and possesses, and commitment to faith is moderated by secularity, but only a real spirituality cemented with bonds of undying devotion and love. The strength of his belief that Islam is indeed, the perfect and modern religion answering the needs of the age, that it requires no modifications to make it workable or complete, and that in its practice one indeed actualises oneself to achieve spirituality, prosperity and perfectness, enables him to advance its message with intense conviction. His deep tolerance and knowledge that the essentials of the faith are not lost in its diverse manifestations in changing climates and cultures, gives him the unique ability to integrate the diverse qualities of his followers who live all over the world and bring their own cultural influences to the community into its collective sociological wealth. He recognises and acknowledges the universality of moral value and the possibility of a pluralism of values existing concurrently with the uniformity of Islam. His confidence in the resilience of its practice enables him to encourage his followers to assimilate the intellectual bounties of our times with an enthusiasm and vigour that has promoted their growth in all fields.

In Syedna Mohammed Burhanuddin, one is moved, above all, with the intensity of his devotion to Imām Husain, whose martyrdom he has given a paradigmatic importance. His undiluted allegiance to the family of the Prophet, who laid down their own lives for the cause of Islam, creates an epic dimension to his call to the faith, resulting in thousands being drawn to him, recognising that in answering his call, they actually respond to the original invitation of Islam. With this, the difficulties of ideology, adherence and practice become surmountable, even in the midst of daunting philosophical scepticism.

The names of the Prophet
Mohammed ﷺ and Ali ؏ in
Kufi script. Al-Aqmar, Cairo.

AN ISLAMIC
IDENTITY

'O Mankind! We have created you male and female, and have made you communities and families that you may know one another. The noblest among you in the sight of Allah is the best in the conduct; Allah is the All-Knowing, the Aware.'

AL-QUR'AN 49:13

'Our teachings lay stress on the mental and material wellbeing, spiritual training, organisational ability and internal discipline of our followers. We have always advised them that they be sincere in their hearts and live a disciplined life, be loyal to the country of their adoption and benefit it through their efforts. In their work, practice, trade and business, they be such citizens as set an example to their neighbours, brothers in faith and fellow-citizens. Their worldly achievements must be designed to be part of their endeavours for the realisation of the life hereafter. The impact of these teachings must be manifest in the individual and social life of our community.'

SYEDNA MOHAMMED BURHANUDDIN

AN ISLAMIC IDENTITY

T HE NEED TO BELONG to a society and have a relevant social cause to identify with, has always been necessary for human groups, but to maintain traditions and values, while simultaneously being relevant to the current milieu is a post-modern imperative. The post-modern age has seen communities face fierce individualism on the one hand and a global technological and communications revolution on the other, which has eroded even the boundaries of nation-states. This has caused traditional communities to undergo a reassessment of identity that is more sweeping in nature than any needed in the past.

The task of a leader in the contemporary age has been to guide his followers through this upheaval of circumstance and remould and re-equip his community to combine the essentials of its tradition with the best that modernity has to offer, without succumbing to destructive assimilation or the ruinous rejection of the age.

At the turn of the 14th Islamic century, in 1399/1978–9, Syedna Mohammed Burhanuddin ﷺ initiated a programme to reinforce the Islamic identity that was the essence of the community. A historic conference called *al-Multaqā al-Fāṭimī al-'Ilmī* was assembled in Al-Jamea-tus-Saifiyah, Surat, India, towards the end of 1978 in which delegates were guided by Syedna to reassess the community's identity and thus determine the direction that the community would take in the future. An attempt was made to identify core values and traditions and investigate the sources of their corruption that debilitated confidence. An identity had to be found from within the community's tradition which would be fully functional in the present. A way had to be found to embrace modernity wholeheartedly without compromising the essentials of any such assertion of selfhood, and without being stranded in the void between modernity and tradition. To this end, the *Multaqā* successfully charted a programme to re-orient the community towards its Islamic roots in all aspects of life and re-assert its Islamic identity in the new Islamic century.

An Islamic identity, it is generally agreed, consists of norms that are manifest in external action that society perceives as distinctly Islamic, which amongst other things requires the dress, appearance, etiquette and behaviour favoured by the *sharī'ah*. For its adherents it must induce a sense of belonging to the Islamic community, without the need to separate themselves from the larger society, so that a wholehearted involvement in public affairs is possible. It must not be cosmetic but must guide the individual and the community to a clearly defined way of life, including the promotion of moral standards, ethical mores and business attitudes, entirely based on Islam.

For individuals the requirement was to own and commit to the religion and its traditions, find the strength to do so from the religion itself, reinforce beliefs by the practice of the faith and validate the faith by its practice. The commitment had to be total to effect the required change. It was either this, or an assimilation into the various antithetical mainstreams of the world with the consequent loss of Islamic values.

In the last twenty years, the genius of this guidance of Syedna Mohammed Burhanuddin ﷺ has been validated. The community has grown and prospered, equally at home with values of tradition and modernity, to exist on par with any other in this challenging era.

The conference, *al-Multaqā al-Fāṭimī al-'Ilmī* held in the *īwān* of Al-Jamea-tus-Saifiyah, Surat on 30th Muḥarram 1399 (29th December 1978) marked the turning point for the community, defining the direction for the community in contemporary times. Syedna had said in his opening address that the conference was destined to be historic, one that would "open the gates to guidance."

A Believer

'Our leaders have taught us that: An ideal believer will have the following virtues,
which are the goals of every human being:

Conviction in religion, firmness in gentleness, craving for knowledge, maturity in learning, frugality in richness, humility in worship, grace in poverty, patience in adversity, pursuit of the lawful.... He engages in good action, is wary of wrong doing. He practices what he professes. His day begins with remembrance of the Creator and ends in giving thanks to Him.... He is enamoured of eternal values and disregards the perishable.'

SYEDNA MOHAMMED BURHANUDDIN ❧ Inaugural address of al-Multaqā al-Fāṭimī al-'Ilmī.

The development of human beings involves rites of passage that mark the spiritual, mental or emotional transition of the person from one stage to another. These rites help define the person's identity in society as he or she moves towards the perceived goals of life. A community such as the Bohras, that owes its existence to its religious heritage has rites of passage that are not only symbolic ritual but infused with spiritual meaning that define an individual's socio-spiritual identity.

The naming ceremony is conducted six days after birth (on the eve of the 7th), by the women in the family. The affirmation of faith and the call to prayer are recited in the child's ears followed by verses of the Qur'an and then the name announced. Parents often request Syedna to choose the name of the child.

Within 21 days of birth, the *'aqīqa* ceremony is performed, in which a sacrificial rite is conducted in a tradition established by the Prophet.

Mīṯāq, undertaken at puberty, marks the child's entry into adulthood. The initiate is asked to affirm his beliefs, establish a covenant with Allah and swear an oath of allegiance to the *imām* and the *imām*'s representative, the *dā'ī*. In so doing, the believer takes upon himself the responsibility of his life's deeds before his Maker.

Nikāḥ, the ceremony of contracting marriage, is a simple ceremony in Islam. The *'āmil* or *qāḍī*, authorised by Syedna, to solemnise the marriage, recites an invocation that is a vital part of the *nikāḥ*. He then guides the groom and a male representative of the bride into making the marriage commitments in accordance with the tenets of the religion. The ceremony's simplicity belies its importance in creating a stable social fabric in the community. Syedna encourages Bohras to marry young and shoulder the responsibilities of a family early in life and has encouraged the formation of organisations all over the world that facilitate the coming together of potential betrothals. Dowry is never proferred.

A community tradition called *Rasm-e-Sayfī* facilitates the *nikāḥ* and creates a collective spirit of celebration by encouraging many couples to come together for the ceremony, though the *nikāḥ* itself is performed separately for each couple. Syedna often conducts such marriages himself.

Dress Etiquette

A person's appearance makes a statement. It is the first aspect of his personality that interacts with society and defines his position within it. It expresses the values and belief system he lives by and enables the people he meets to know the options of life he has chosen. A Muslim wears loose clothing that befits his lifestyle and facilitates the five obligatory prayers that he performs during the day. The clothes are designed to express a modesty in both men and women in conformity to the *sharī'ah* and show their status of responsibility in Allah's creation.

Intrapsychically, on the other hand, one's dress etiquette has the ability to alter one's thinking and feeling and become a major component of one's identity. Syedna Mohammed Burhanuddin has emphasised that Bohra men should adhere to the practice of the Prophet of growing a full beard and also wear the *topi* (traditional cap). Women, for their part, should don the traditional all-covering garb called *ridā'*, in keeping with the dignity of women defined by Islam. In an era of a plethora of cultures and value-systems, made available to all through mass communication, the possibility of losing one's cultural moorings has never been greater. A sharp identity engendered by a dress code has allowed the community to focus on Islamic traditions in a powerful way.

Prayer is the cornerstone of all Islamic practice. Congregations gather daily in *masjid*s and other community centres to offer the five prayers obligatory in Islam. The benefit of greeting and meeting each other is a natural social gain that accompanies the practice.

In the month of Ramaḍān, every Bohra engages in daylong fasts accompanied by increased recitation of the Qurʾan and supplications that make the month a season of piety. The fasts are normally broken with a communal meal after sunset. Syedna gives particular attention to the religious obligations of his followers during this month, ensuring that someone with the right abilities is sent to lead prayers and impart religious knowledge to even the remotest of areas where only a handful of Bohras may live. More established centres are sent learned graduates of Al-Jamea-tus-Saifiyah to conduct a specific educational course (called *niṣāb al-barakāt*) over the month. Such endeavours enable Bohras all over the world to undertake their religious obligations during the auspicious month in a fruitful way.

It is also common practice to offer *zakāh* annually during the month of Ramaḍān. This obligation, the giving of a portion of one's retained wealth to the cause of Allah in recognition of Him as the Provider is one of the fundamental principles of Islam. The Bohra community has always adhered to this principle, but in recent years, the practice has been greatly enhanced, with offerings made with greater dedication.

The *majlis* is an age-old tradition in which Dawoodi Bohras gather for the remembrance (*zikr*) of Allah. It is conducted in a well-defined form and a specific sequence of recitation developed over the centuries, and is held on the important dates of the Islamic calendar. Besides their religious significance, such gatherings engender a social togetherness that fosters a spirit of fellowship and brotherhood. In a special form of the *majlis*, called the *waʿz majlis*, an orator delivers a sermon which may last up to 3 hours. When Syedna delivers his, as seen here in Udaipur, thousands sit in rapt silence to imbibe every word, in a tradition that takes one back a thousand years.

Strengths of the Community

The Dawoodi Bohra Community is known for its discipline. This discipline arises from the acceptance of the central authority of the *dāʿī* that is pivotal to their faith and from the personal discipline that Islam fosters in each believer. This in turn allows other worthy characteristics to be cultivated, including the sense of abiding by the law of the land. Islam requires of its adherents to love the land of their abode as part of their faith. The community is thus law-abiding and peace-loving, having conscientiously abstained from subversion or destruction, abhorring violence. Another characteristic that discipline fosters is self-reliance, which in turn promotes a business sense that the community is known for.

The Bohra community, like any other traditional community, has a strong sense of family values developed from their religious sentiments. These values, nuclear in nature but espousing the virtues of an extended family, have provided a sturdy source of stability against the onslaught of urban modernity which often destroys the fabric of the family in favour of individual independence.

Islam's insistence on education and the various educational programmes fostered by Syedna have ensured nearly a hundred percent literacy rate within the community.

One of the major strengths of the community is its language, *lisān al-daʿwah*. This language was developed when the mission first came to Gujarat through missionaries from the Fatimi Empire about a thousand years ago. *Lisān al-daʿwah* takes its basic syntax and structure from the Gujarati language but a large part of its vocabulary and its script is Arabic. Like Urdu, these elements give it an Islamic dimension that has allowed the transmission of Qurʾanic and Arabic values to a people distant from the land of Arabia. To the community, it has given a medium to articulate its religion and heritage whilst simultaneously allowing it to continue with the language and norms of the land of their abode. Arabic continues to be the community's language for religious works and literature, the language aspired to by the learned, but *lisān al-daʿwah* is its language of sermons and its medium of official and day-to-day communication. Whilst the Qurʾanic purity of the Arabic used in the community is maintained, *lisān al-daʿwah* is an ever-evolving language adopting terms and phrases from the current linguistic milieu that give it a contemporary expression.

Another unique feature of the community is its calendar. Widely used in the Fatimi Empire, it is based on the 29.5 day lunar cycle with appropriate compensations in the form of leap years. Its accuracy has been validated by its use over a millennium. The calendar's efficacy and its value in the present situation with the community spread all over the globe has been to provide it with clearly identified dates for its celebrations and commemorations that have in turn united the community in its religious practices.

Joining each other for meals is a particularly well-known Dawoodi Bohra custom. Families and friends gather around sharing the meal from a single large raised circular tray called *thāl*. The custom strengthens the family unit and the sense of solidarity between the people eating together, increases the pleasure of the meal and creates a shared sense of the blessing received from Allah. Seen above is a personal glimpse of Syedna sharing a meal with his sons and grandchildren.

Even in small communities, physically distant from the community's hub in India, where the congregation in a particular town may number only a few dozen, the maintenance of tradition, culture and values is given priority. A community centre is purchased and an organisation set up to cater for such needs. Seen here is the congregation of Manchester, UK, comprising about 300 adults and children, in a typical Dawoodi Bohra *majlis*.

The Administrative System of Dawat-e-Hadiyah

Though a minority community in every land, Dawoodi Bohras have successfully preserved their identity, tradition and cultural heritage. An identification with the aspirations and obligations implicit in their attachment to their land of abode has never proved incompatible with the practice of their religion and the maintaining of their religious heritage. This sustaining of religiosity and dedication to their historical legacy has been possible in no small measure through an elaborate administrative system set up by the central organisation of the *dā'ī*, called Dawat-e-Hadiyah.

Syedna appoints a functionary called an *'āmil* in every town where a sizeable group of Bohras reside. This institution is age-old, being part of the Fatimi administrative system. The *'āmil* administers and manages the socio-religious affairs of the local community, called the *jamā'at*, as its head. He derives his authority to function directly from Syedna and it is this authority that provides the doctrinal endorsement to his activities in the *jamā'at*. The affairs of the *jamā'at* are administered by a committee called an *anjuman* presided over by the *'āmil*. The *anjuman* operates under a constitution granted by Syedna and procures and maintains communal institutions such as a *masjid*, a *jamā'at-khāna* where socio-religious functions are performed, *madrasa*s where children are given religious education, schools and cemeteries. Often other organisations operate under the *anjuman* that cater for specific needs, such as the aspirations of the young. These organisations serve the local community, help maintain a fellowship and brotherhood and become the vehicles for promoting welfare within the community under the overall guidance from the central office of Syedna. From time to time, this organisational set-up is augmented by special emissaries of Syedna, who perform specific duties, give a fresh look at all the organisations of the local community, attend to personal needs of individuals and clarify Syedna's edicts in social and religious affairs.

India is home to historical centres of Dawoodi Bohras. These centres mainly comprise of cities such as Ahmedabad and Surat, from which the *dā'ī*s operated. Mumbai is now the main centre, being home to the central office of Syedna and the largest Bohra population. More recent settlements have taken place in many other major cities all across India, such as Chennai and Calcutta. India currently has 215 Dawoodi Bohra *jamā'ats* each operating under an *'āmil* and hundreds of other smaller ones that operate under a *wālī mullā* appointed by Syedna from amongst the local congregation. Yemen has 23 *jamā'ats*. There are hundreds of other Dawoodi Bohra congregations all over the world, from Sydney to San Francisco, about 75 of which are full-fledged *jamā'ats* each led by an *'āmil*.

The organisational structure and administrative framework derived from the Fatimi system and developed by the *dā'ī*s over the centuries has been efficacious to the Bohras, allowing them to be comfortable with contemporary internationalism and transcend international boundaries whilst maintaining their strong bond with the *dā'ī* of the time. Religion is perceived as a stabilising and uniting agency, a mortar to the brotherhood of man rather than a barrier. Their reverence for the *dā'ī* and their belief in the efficacy of his authority has engendered the smooth running of an administrative system that continues to nourish their fellowship to this day.

The Dawoodi Bohra society has been carefully structured by successive *dāʿīs* to enable every individual to find his place within it by providing a function and a role for everyone. These functions are both linked and independent, allowing a sense of society to exist without making the operation of any group dependent on another. The child imbibes the values of his society as well as the skills he requires to find his place in the larger world. The adults have personal, domestic and commercial obligations of their own, but all of them – men, women and children – are always given the opportunity, within the community organisations, of finding the greater fulfilment of participating in social tasks that are larger than those of individual lives.

The community's spirit of service (*khidmat*) is inculcated as a valued deed of merit and channelled through numerous organisations such as Shababul Eidiz Zahabi for young men, Bunaiyatul Eidiz Zahabi and Burhani Women's Association for women. Students join Talebat al-Kulliyatil Muminaat for girls and Tolaba al-Kulliyatil Muminoon for boys. These organisations serve the community and the public at large.

The Status of Women

It is said that the philosophy that guides a human society is not better judged than in the way in which women function within it. Islam defines specific rights for women, for example, in education and in the ownership of property; and the administrative and judicial framework of the Bohra society ensures that these rights are always upheld. Syedna Mohammed Burhanuddin particularly ensures that the education of girls is promoted at par with the education of boys. Dawoodi Bohra women thus have an equal access and opportunity to educational, religious or social occasions in the community and enjoy full participation in its activities.

At the same time the community is deeply conscious of the changing demands that modernity makes on the woman and her own changing expectations of life and opportunities. Women are encouraged to make an active contribution to the societies they live in. This they do in a variety of ways, which includes the pursuit of socially and intellectually demanding professions such as medicine or education. However, Syedna makes it imperative upon them to ensure that neither their dignity nor their independence is compromised by their occupations. Islamic decorum is observed by the *ḥijāb* (veil), that in being worn, also establishes the values that the Dawoodi Bohra woman chooses to live by.

Traditional gender roles are never disparaged and the woman's contribution in the happiness and functioning of the home acknowledged with both respect and gratitude. The role of the woman as a home-maker is regarded as critical in the healthy upbringing of the family and one which is essential to the wellbeing of the community as a whole. The historical lore of the community is replete with examples of brave and articulate women who even while playing vital roles in the running of the state, tended to their husbands, homes and children with equal interest and no loss of stature. The integration that has consequently been fostered over generations in the personality of the Dawoodi Bohra woman today, is both viable and inspiring as any sociological scrutiny reveals.

Several informal and formal organisations ranging from a structured circle of a few intimate friends, to larger organisations that run into a hundred or more allow a close bonding to take place between women. They are supported by each other in the goals they set themselves within the parameters they live in, and find through their activities and endeavours, their place in the sisterhood of all women.

Amatullah Aisaheba, the late wife of Syedna, set a contemporary paradigm of Islamic womanhood for the community. Immersing herself in the welfare of individuals, she worked tirelessly yet unobtrusively, dwelling on their concerns with the compassion and detail that a mother brings to the task. She published several books of prayer and instructions on the performance of religious rites from which the community has benefited immensely. She is still remembered and cherished and her resting place in London is regularly visited by Bohras.

Restored 12th century Fatimi
design. Al-Aqmar, Cairo

TOWARDS
ISLAMIC
SOCIO-ECONOMICS

اَلْخَلْقُ عِيَالُ اللهِ

وَاَحَبُّ الْخَلْقِ اِلَى اللهِ تَعَالَىٰ اَنْفَعُهُمْ لِعِيَالِهِ،

'Mankind is a single family dependent on Allah and most beloved
to Allah is one who is most beneficial to it.'

MOHAMMED RASULULLAH ﷺ

'Justice and benevolence are the two great principles of faith.
When mercy assists justice, a peaceful society comes into
existence. Faith invites us towards a noble character so that we
may create on earth a virtuous society which ensures the welfare
and happiness of the masses and the prosperity of nations.'

SYEDNA MOHAMMED BURHANUDDIN ❀

TOWARDS ISLAMIC SOCIO-ECONOMICS

BEING a complete way of life, Islam does not recognise a separation of spheres of operation between the material and spiritual aspects of man's life. Toiling for the material benefit of the family and society becomes an act of worship, provided that the effort to earn a living does not make one negligent of Allah as the real Provider. Islam has praised the practice of trade and business just as it has denounced the injustices of interest. The importance of trade has been inculcated in Dawoodi Bohras by their leaders over the centuries, insisting that there is more honour in earning a small living while working for oneself than living a life of luxury in the service of others. Self-employment instils a reliance on Allah, whereas working for others creates the illusion that the employer is the benefactor. Thus, over the years, the Bohras have acquired a strong tradition of self-employment, trade and business. Indeed the word Bohra is itself a derivative of the term "trader" in Gujarati.

This tradition of business has come under renewed threat in the modern business environment that is significantly un-Islamic. The economic paradigms applicable to an Islamic community encompass a wider range of issues than merely the generation of wealth and equitable distribution. They are based upon socio-economic justice and overall human wellbeing, which in some cases conflicts with mainstream economic paradigms of self-interest and competition in an open market. Interest plays a central role in the dominating economic system by defining the value, means and ethics of borrowing, from personal finance to macro-economics. This interest-permeated economy is in disharmony with Islam, which considers interest as inherently unjust. Amongst the many differing opinions of modern economists, one analysis is that interest engenders a system which disadvantages the less well-off at an individual level as well as in the economic relations between nations. That it has the characteristics of strengthening the idle custodians of capital (banks) at the expense of the entrepreneurs who are the true wealth creators. However, despite its disadvantages, interest-based finance is so well entrenched within the machinery of modern economics and such is its lure, that it was until the last few decades, unthinkable to seek a more just and a more Islamic alternative.

The task of re-orienting a community towards an Islamic socio-economic system in contemporary times is thus a major undertaking. It entails a radical restructuring of business attitudes and ethics. Nevertheless, to re-orient the Dawoodi Bohra Community was a challenge Syedna Mohammed Burhanuddin ❀ had to take up as part of the reaffirmation to the principles by which the community had lived throughout its history. He asked his community to rally behind two economic principles of Islam. The first being to recognise interest in all its forms as *ḥarām*, that is, sinful and morally wrong. The taking and the giving and any sort of dealing in interest was to be eschewed even if it made apparent business sense, and even if economic pressures demanded it. The second was to recognise the merits of *qarḍan ḥasanā* (literally "good loan"), or interest-free loan. Loans so given transformed a material transaction to a spiritual one, the merits of which exceeded that of charity. These principles would transform a business activity that might otherwise attract sin and immorality to one of virtue and merit. Whilst recognising that these two principles on their own do not cover all the aspects of an Islamic financial system these steps were perceived to be critical in planning an Islamic socio-economy for the community.

Ever since 1979, when the call was first made in the historic conference, *al-Multaqā al-Fāṭimī al-'Ilmī*, the community took firm measures to stop all dealings in interest. Huge businesses that depended on bank loans were restructured, new enterprises were started on an equity-sharing basis and funds were set up to offer *qarḍan ḥasanā*. Syedna set up a number of trusts and institutions with the aim of offering such loans. These measures revolutionised the way in which businesses and finance operated in the community, but more importantly, it revolutionised the attitude towards wealth, self-reliance and assistance to fellow men. Money now circulates within the community on an interest-free basis in the belief that the provider of the funds is the one to whom the favour is being done by the borrower.

The economic growth in the community since these measures were put into practice has surpassed all expectations. The community has not only grown in enterprise and philanthropy, but has undertaken more projects than ever before for the charitable benefit of the community and humanity at large.

Syedna has encouraged charity, a fundamental practice of Islam, in a way that is meaningful. Man must be taught to care for his neighbours as a necessity. Real charity is one in which the lot of the receiver is improved permanently without him feeling the pangs of indignity. For such charitable work, Syedna has established a number of trusts and organisations, each with specific objectives to provide assistance in a particular area. Some of them are targeted to education, others to the environment, others to relief of poverty and yet others to the promotion of women's enterprises. The Amatullah Aaisaheba Memorial Trust started in 1996, for example, has been set up for the particular assistance of women's enterprises.

One of the sessions of *al-Multaqā al-Fāṭimī al-'Ilmī* in
1399/1978–79 which earmarked the community's resolve to
develop a business ethic based on the prohibition of interest.

In 1405/1985, to commemorate the 1400th birth anniversary of Imām al-Husain and the 100th birth anniversary of
Syedna Taher Saifuddin, a 5-point programme was launched reinforcing the landmark decisions of *al-Multaqā al-
Fāṭimī al-'Ilmī*. It called for a recommitment to all the principles of the *sharī'ah* of Islam and to an honouring of its
traditions. It sought to make Islamic education the basis of acquiring all knowledge. It established *qarḍan ḥasanā* as
the principle upon which the economic progress of the individual and the community was based and urged the
community to strive for a livelihood in ways permissible and recommended by Islam. And finally, it impelled them
to embark upon widespread deeds of welfare and philanthropy.

The Institutionalisation of Qarḍan Ḥasanā

Qarḍan ḥasanā organisations and trusts established by Syedna have provided an impetus for the community's economic restructuring. These trusts maintain a uniformity of operation all over the world and base their lending on strict guidelines, fixing the term of the loan, scrutinising applications, advising the applicant on the viability of the project, securing the loan with a reasonable security and guarantors and extending the loan period when necessary. That this worldly exercise is a religious command, attracting celestial blessings, permeates and dominates its procedures.

These guidelines, based meticulously on Islamic principles have engendered an economic activity that is nothing short of having institutionalised the concept of *qarḍan ḥasanā*. Hundreds of *qarḍan ḥasanā* organisations now exist in Canada, Egypt, Far East, India, Kenya, Kuwait, Madagascar, Malaysia, Pakistan, Sri Lanka, Tanzania, U.A.E., UK and USA where Bohras live, and have a corpus in excess of millions. Even towns with the smallest Bohra population run a *qarḍan ḥasanā* programme.

The principal beneficiaries of these schemes have been Bohras who intend to enter into business for the first time followed by those who need to borrow to expand their businesses or finance a new venture. *Qarḍan ḥasanā* is also available for all other types of personal borrowings.

Excerpts from the Burhani Qarḍan Ḥasanā Trust (India) Deed

PURPOSES:

3.   The trust is established for the following public non-communal charitable purposes and shall be administered without regard to caste, colour or creed:

3.1.   To promote, encourage and assist in giving of qarḍan ḥasanā (interest free loans) to those deserving.

3.2.   To serve as an agency to those who wish to give qarḍan ḥasanā (interest free loans) individually or collectively.

3.3.   To give qarḍan ḥasanā (interest free loans) either to or through an institution or body of individuals on such terms and conditions as the trustees for the time being in office may determine from time to time.

3.4.   The relief of poverty including the establishment, maintenance and support of institutions or funds for the relief of the poor by way of a loan without interest (qarḍan ḥasanā) for setting up such person in a business or otherwise for the purpose of rehabilitating him.

Burhani Qardan Hasana Trust (India) was formed in 1991 as part of the mass movement to promote the concept of *qarḍan ḥasanā*. This movement has now given rise to similar organisations serving thousands in many countries. As the corpus steadily grows by Syedna adding more and more to the movement at every juncture and occasion, more and more Bohras approach the organisations for loans.

A bore-well at Kauka in Ahmedabad District (ABOVE) activated with an interest-free loan from the Burhani Qardan Hasana Trust, India. The trust provides loans from as little as $20 to as much as $100,000 and benefits a small individual project and a large enterprise alike. Loans granted for agricultural activities make possible the purchase of equipment such as tractors and well pumps (BELOW).

Syedna often visits industries (seen here in India, Kenya and Egypt), owned by industrialists who have restructured their businesses to be free from borrowing on interest. Their progress has inspired others and their prosperity has benefited Bohras through *qarḍan ḥasanā* schemes operated by the community.

Small businesses have often benefited from the interest-free loan schemes operating within the community. Some Mumbai street traders, for example, rely on a regular supply of ready-cash to purchase in bulk, a practice that is essential to their survival in a competitive business. Others borrow to enhance their businesses.

Syedna has set up a number of trusts that foster the spirit of Islamic economic enterprise and welfare. The purpose of such trusts is to aid the needy and deserving in a way that eliminates dependency and encourages self-reliance, thereby breaking the cycle of poverty.

The first such charitable organisation, The Saifee Foundation, was established by Syedna Taher Saifuddin in India in1959. Seen on the left, is Syedna Taher Saifuddin signing the trust deed that has guided the organisation for four decades in its charitable objectives. Since then, many organisations with parallel aims have been formed. The Saifee Foundation Of Europe, for example, formed in London in 1964, has aided educational projects and in recent years has become the focus of *qarḍan ḥasanā* activities of the community in Europe. In addition to the Saifee Foundation, in Kenya and Tanzania, trusts with similar aims and objectives called Burhani Foundation were formed in 1980 and 1985 respectively.

Excerpts from the Saifee Foundation Trust Deed

PURPOSES:

4(a)   The relief of poverty including the establishment, maintenance and support of institutions or funds for the relief of the poor and including any help to any poor person or persons either by way of grant or donation or loan free of interest or in any other manner....

4(b)   The advancement and propagation of education and learning including the establishment, maintenance and support of educational institutions, professorships,.... And the promotion of literature...

4(c)   Medical relief including the establishment and maintenance and support of institutions or funds for such relief, such as hospitals....

4(d)   The advancement and propagation of any other object of a charitable nature beneficial to the public at large.

In 1966, a trust with parallel aims to the Saifee Foundation was set up. Called His Holiness Dr. Syedna Taher Saifuddin Memorial Foundation, this trust has funded and managed hundreds of projects in India, ranging from the purchase of medical and agricultural equipment to providing scholarship and poverty relief. Parallel independent Memorial Foundations were set up in Sri Lanka and Kenya in 1968, Pakistan in 1978 and Tanzania in 1985 for the benefit of the general population.

The Memorial Foundation supports rural projects that improve the quality of life for the people of the area. A water pipeline project in Virdi, for example, which serves local residents, was installed with grants from the trust.

A typical small trader assisted in his business by grants from the trust.

The trust frequently runs child care clinics in schools to provide free dental checkups, eye tests and audiometry screening.

Excerpts from the Burhani Foundation (India) Trust Deed

OBJECTS:

To promote, foster, carry out, aid and assist
      programmes and projects for the conservation
      of the environment and resources of Nature as
      also to promote research and study of the
      same....

To promote and foster concern for environmental
      security, the conservation of the biological
      diversity of the planet and the green
      movement through fuel conservation, optimum
      utilisation of resources, pollution
      management and related measures....

The Burhani Foundation (India) was founded in 1991, making the community focus on environmental concerns, the most pressing issue of the last decades. The preamble of the trust calls upon the human being, endowed with countless blessings, the peak and purpose of Allah's creation, to take his responsibility towards all Allah's creation seriously and care for the earth as one of Allah's special bounties. The trust was launched at a massive gathering of the Bohras at the Turf Club, Mumbai, India, and has successfully completed a number of useful projects in India. It maintains an internet web site that expresses its purpose and programme.

Excerpts from the Amatullah Aaisaheba Memorial Trust Deed (India)

OBJECTS AND PURPOSES:

4.   The promotion and wellbeing of society by providing education, medical relief, relief of poverty or distress and any other object of general public utility without discrimination to caste, creed, religion or sex.

4.1   To promote and assist learning and education in its widest connotation...assisting research programmes in medicine, cancer among women and diseases inflicting children....

4.2   To provide medical relief, including... Support of maternity homes, childcare centres, sanatoriums, aiding maternity cases, prenatal and postnatal care, sponsoring health camps for women and children, care of infants....

4.3   To give relief in poverty and distress, including establishing, maintaining and supporting orphanages, homes for widows and the destitute....

4.4.   ...Aiding and assisting projects for the welfare of humanity in general and women and children in particular....

The Amatullah Aaisaheba Memorial Trust was formed in 1996 in India and Pakistan in memory of the wife of Syedna who passed away in 1994 in London. Epitomising Islamic womanhood, she played a leading role in the welfare of Dawoodi Bohras, particularly that of women. The trust aspires to continue her work.

The trust lays particular emphasis on the support of home industries run by women, such as this, for needlecrafts.

Syedna Mohammed Burhanuddin has encouraged the establishment of hundreds of clinics, child care centres and maternity homes in India, Pakistan and East Africa. They provide medical aid and relief to Dawoodi Bohras and others alike. In addition, well-equipped, full-fledged hospitals have been established in various cities that maintain the highest standards of equipment and organisation and provide nearly free medical care.

A new ambitious project to re-build the Saifee Hospital in the heart of Mumbai is currently underway, occupying 4400 sq. metres (model, RIGHT).

The Nursery and Incubation Control Unit at the Burhani Hospital, Dar-es-Salaam, Tanzania.

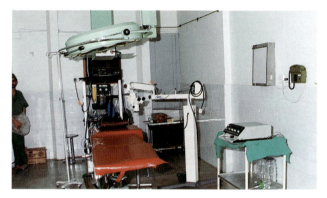

One of the operation theatres of Burhani Hospital, Karachi, Pakistan.

Saifee Ambulance in Mumbai, India, provides invaluable, subsidised medical services to the local neighbourhood. These include post hospitalisation help, immunisations, and blood donations. The organisation also often sets up camps for specialised medical services.

The Bohras benefit from numerous organisations run voluntarily by dedicated workers. Hizbul Huda, in Mumbai, for example, attends to the funeral rites of the deceased, easing the burden of the bereaved. Another organisation called Anjuman-e-Mutatawain distributes grain to the needy in Mumbai.

The community organises schemes to facilitate the purchase of flats and houses, at subsidised rates. Such schemes attempt to establish a mixed residency by ensuring that whilst most houses are bought by those who can afford them, some in the neighbourhood are occupied by the less well-off. Grants and gifts are often offered to the deserving to facilitate this residency requirement, and in some cases, houses are offered freely to the deserving.

Housing complex in Kalyan, Mumbai, India.

Housing complex in Marol, Mumbai, India.

Housing complex in Nairobi, Kenya.

This housing complex in Jamnagar, India was built by Syedna specifically to house the less well-off. The residents are charged no rent and only contribute towards the maintenance of the building.

One of the most noteworthy and comprehensive facilities provided by institutions established by the past *dā'īs* is that of looking after the needs of pilgrims and travellers. There is virtually no pilgrimage site and no city with a sizeable population of Dawoodi Bohras, which does not have a *musāfirkhāna* (rest house). These *musāfirkhāna*s not only provide a welcome subsidised shelter for the pilgrim or traveller but also extend the hospitalities normally due to a traveller under Islamic norms. The pilgrim is invited to meals three times a day and food is cooked to cater for the hundreds who may be present.

Syedna Taher Saifuddin built al-Maḥall al-Sayfī in Makkah al-Mukarrama in 1344/1925. This magnificent building, ideally positioned near the holy Ka'ba, has served the pilgrims for years. An organisation called Fayz-e-Hashimi caters for their needs and looks after al-Maḥall al-Sayfī. Due to the increased number of pilgrims each year, a new rest house is being built.

Excerpts from the Fayz-e-Husayni Trust Deed

OBJECTS :

3.1   To foster and promote the performance of *hajj, umrah and ziyarah and to aid and assist pilgrims in such performance*....

3.2   To provide amenities, facilities and guidance for pilgrims....

3.3   To arrange *niyaz* (food) and feed, house and accommodate pilgrims and for this purpose to lease, let and engage *musafirkhanas* (rest homes), hotels....

3.4   To provide *khidmat* (service) to pilgrims as specified by al-Dai al-Mutlaq....

3.5   To help any deserving Muslim to carry out his religious obligations as prescribed by Islam.

Fayz-e-Husayni was formed in 1303/1882 by the 48th *dā'ī*, Syedna AbdulHusain Husamuddin with the task of catering for the needs of pilgrims. It has served pilgrims for over a hundred years, looking after their travel requirements and setting up rest-houses in a number of places, including the principal pilgrimage sites in Madina, Najaf and Kerbala. This organisation has been greatly expanded by Syedna to meet the requirements of travellers today. A number of sister organisations such as Fayz-e-Hakimi in Cairo and Damascus and Fayz-e-Hatimi in Yemen perform similar duties.

ABOVE The Fayz-e-Husayni rest house in al-Madina al-Munawwara, Saudi Arabia.

ABOVE RIGHT The Fayz-e-Husayni rest house in Karbala, Iraq.

RIGHT The Fayz-e-Hatymi rest house in Sanaa, Yemen, serves pilgrims visiting the various pilgrimage sites in Yemen.

BELOW LEFT The rest house in Ujjain, India, forms part of the complex that has a *masjid* and a mausoleum over the graves of three *dāʿī*s.

BELOW RIGHT The Manazil-e-Hakimiyah rest house in Burhanpur, India, serves thousands who visit the pilgrimage site each year.

The "Verse of Purity" attributed to the close family
of the Prophet, written around the names of
Mohammed ﷺ and Ali ؑ. Al-Aqmar, Cairo.

A DIVINE
LOVE

اِنِّيْ تَارِكٌ فِيْكُمُ الثَّقَلَيْنِ كِتَابَ اللهِ وَعِتْرَتِيْ
مَا اِنْ تَمَسَّكْتُمْ بِهِمَا لَنْ تَضِلُّوْا بَعْدِيْ.

'I leave behind two precious things, the Book of Allah and my progeny.
As long as you hold fast to them both, you will not go astray.'

MOHAMMED RASULULLAH ﷺ

'We love Mohammed ﷺ only because of our
love of Allah and we love his progeny only because of our love
for Mohammed ﷺ.'

SYEDNA MOHAMMED BURHANUDDIN
QUOTING THE IMAMS

A DIVINE LOVE

*T*AQWĀ, a delicate feeling of love, awe and fear of Allah, the Merciful, the Beneficent, is the most profound sentiment in Islam. The Creator, in all His unknowability, in all His sublimity and in all His might is to be loved as if He were the closest to one's being. Facets of *taqwā* can be evidenced and experienced readily by love for Allah's chosen prophets, messengers and those whom He has favoured with His closeness. The last of the prophets and their seal and leader, Mohammed al-Muṣṭafā ☙, emphasised the importance of this love as a fundamental principle of faith.

Thus, as a requisite part of the faith, the Prophet and his successors from amongst his progeny, the *imām*s, are revered and loved. Their teachings are learned and imbibed. Their sacrifices for the sake of Allah are remembered and their lives made paradigms for the lives of the common man. The Prophet and his immediate family, his daughter, Fatima ☙, his successor, Ali ibn Abi Talib ☙ and their two sons Imām Hasan ☙ and Imām Husain ☙ are specially esteemed. Syedna Mohammed Burhanuddin ☙ has defined this love as a consequence of the love a believer has for Allah.

Syedna has always emphasised the great debt mankind owes to Imām Husain ☙, who sacrificed himself and his family for values that mankind holds dear. He has said that this debt must not for a moment be forgotten and that esteem and reverence for it will inculcate in human beings the best of values and qualities and will inspire steadfastness on the path of Allah. That this remembrance and love will transcend prejudices and extend to the love of creation as a whole, which as the Prophet said, attracts the reciprocal love of Allah.

This message is conveyed through the tradition of remembering and mourning Imām Husain ☙ and the family of the Prophet over the first days of Muḥarram leading to 'Āshūrā'. This age-old tradition has been raised to unprecedented levels by Syedna Mohammed Burhanuddin ☙. Each year, thousands, even hundreds of thousands gather to hear him recount the heart-rending sacrifice, and with it expound upon the mysteries of faith. Thousands more listen to his discourses throughout the world where these discourses are relayed. The logistics of gathering thousands, accommodating them, feeding them and seating them to hear the discourses properly are formidable. Often, only a few days notice is given to the host city to make its preparations. The community all over the world mobilises itself to make the journey, indeed, a pilgrimage.

Another expression of the love for the family of the Prophet is by visiting their burial places in an act of pilgrimage. Syedna has fabricated and dedicated sepulchres (*maqṣūras*) at a number of sites in Iraq, Syria, Jordan and Egypt where the faithful go as humble pilgrims to pay their respects. Such is the regard for the honour of adorning these pilgrimage sites that the entire community is moved by the installations and the inauguration events are reverentially remembered for years.

'We mourn your father al-Husain who chose martyrdom.

O our leaders, do glance at our tears of grief'.

نَبْكِي الْحُسَيْنَ شَهِيدَ الطَّفِّ وَالِدَكُمْ

فَلْتَنْظُرُوا سَادَتِيْ اَدْمُعَنَا الْجَازِعَة

'Our caravans journey towards you, with the

Standards of our love raised high as we approach you'.

تَسْرِيْ قَوَافِلُنَا قَاصِلَةً نَحْوَكُمْ

اَعْلَامَ حُبِّكُمْ فِيْ سَيْرِهَا رَافِعَة

Two couplets from a heart rending composition addressing the *imāms*, the progeny of the Prophet, written by Syedna Mohammed Burhanuddin.

The Sacrifice of Imām Husain

About fifty years after the death of the Prophet, the rulership of the Islamic world was wrested by Yazid ibn Muawiya, who claimed to be the head of State and represent the authority of Islam and yet had no love or patience for the religion. He flouted every precept of Islam and dealt severely with the surviving companions of the Prophet who had remained pious. The Muslims were aghast but confusion reigned the day and they were unable to check the disbelief and impiety that was spreading through the fabric of the community. At this critical juncture, Imām Husain, the grandson of the Prophet, decided to lay down his life to save Islam from sure destruction and to uphold the cherished values of mankind. This selfless act was enacted on the plains of Karbala in 61/680, when he and his loyal men, numbering seventy two, were surrounded by thousands of Yazid's soldiers, kept without food and water for 3 days, and then on the day of 'Āshūrā', massacred, one by one. Even a six month old son of Imām Husain was not spared. This event became a focal point around which the Muslims rallied, jolted from their apathy, and the truth of the divine message was rescued from being extinguished. The word 'Āshūrā', even today, evokes powerful sentiments of selflessness and sacrifice of Imām Husain, the greatest martyr of Islam and its saviour; and his sacrifice continues, 1400 years later, to move the hardest of hearts to tears.

No site evokes a greater emotion
than a large gathering listening
intently to the heart-rending
account of Imām Husain's
martyrdom and manifesting their
grief and lamentation. The
atmosphere is undoubtedly
augmented by the size of the
gathering which can run into
hundreds of thousands. Even the
walls embellished with calligraphic
verses speak of the epic event and
the love for the Prophet and his
family. The discourses are a
treasury of knowledge for the
listeners. The mourning that
accompanies these tales of great
sacrifices revives with poetic
passion the experience in the their
hearts, through which the sacrifice
transcends historical narrative.

This *majlis* held in Ghurratul
Masajid, Mumbai, in 1415/1994
was relayed live to all other local
masjids in Mumbai to a total of
about 150,000 people.

Majlis views at Indore in 1986 (BELOW LEFT) which was attended by about 250,000 people and in Surat (LEFT AND BELOW) in 1997 during the opening of al-Masjid al-Muazzam which drew 150,000. Bohra women participate equally in all religious rites with the upper floors of masjids being reserved for them.

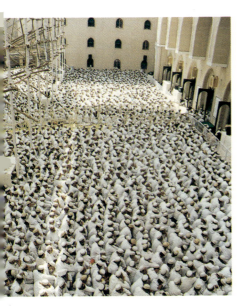

The Tradition of 'Ashara Majlis

The *majlis*, literally gathering, like the well-known Friday *khutba* is a deeply rooted Islamic tradition. Formalised by the Fatimi Imāms, the *majlis* aims to call one towards Allah, to educate and elucidate, to inspire and mobilise. The *'ashara majlis* is a distinct form of *majlis* that recapitulates the supreme sacrifice of Imām Husain and the events of Karbala. It exudes the highest form of spirituality and serves to impart the deepest forms of exegesis and philosophy to the gathering.

The *majlis* can be said to consist of two components. The first is the discourse (*wa'ẓ*), which summons the faithful to Allah, in the words of the Qur'an, "with wisdom and good counsel". The discourse invokes the love of the Prophet and his close family and recounts their sacrifices to strengthen the resolve of the faithful in imbibing the values of the martyrs. It also instructs and educates on the faith of Islam, and narrates with love and devotion, the inspiring history of the prophets, *imāms* and *dā'ī*s.

Formal lament, articulated by the devotees as a result of being moved by the discourse is the second component of the *majlis*. The lament is expressed by weeping and by *mātam*, that is manifesting grief by beating one's breast. It is also expressed by the rhetorical recitation of an elegy, called *marsiya*, delivered devotionally. These are formal "rites of remembrance" of Imām Husain and form part of the traditional mourning of his martyrdom.

The *majlis* has developed a structure, whereby the *wā'iẓ*, the one who delivers the discourse, sits on a *takht* (sermon seat) before the listeners who maintain a specific decorum and sit in a defined order. The *wā'iẓ* begins his discourse with a structured sequence of recitations, which form an exordium. The discourse itself is also carefully sequenced but allows ample room for spontaneity of address. As the *wā'iẓ* recounts the poignant narrative, the audience participate by open lament and the *'ashara majlis* takes the participant through the hearing of a discourse into an experience of spiritual catharsis.

As soon as the venue for *'ashara* (the 10-day period) is known, teams set up camp and begin the colossal preparatory work. A temporary floor or two is added to the *masjid* to create more room. A platform is built outside to effectively extend its floor space, an air-cooling system is constructed, entry and exit gates built for traffic flow, medical teams and checkpoints set up. Accommodation and food teams gather their data and resource pools. The teams have to work round the clock to complete the work in time. As the guests arrive, accommodation is allocated and seating designated. All efforts, entirely voluntary, are directed towards a single aim – to extend every courtesy and cater for every need of the participant.

The venues for Syedna's *'ashara* discourses have been

1386/1966	*Mumbai, India*
1387/1967	*Mumbai, India*
1388/1968	*Mumbai, India*
1389/1969	*Makkah, Saudi Arabia*
1390/1970	*Colombo, Sri Lanka*
1391/1971	*Culcutta, India*
1392/1972	*Surat, India*
1393/1973	*Mumbai, India*
1394/1974	*Mumbai, India*
1395/1975	*Mumbai, India*
1396/1976	*Culcutta, India*
1397/1976	*Chennai, India*
1398/1977	*Karachi, Pakistan*
1399/1978	*Jamnagar, India*
1400/1979	*Mumbai, India*
1401/1980	*Cairo, Egypt*
1402/1981	*Cairo, Egypt*
1403/1982	*Sidhpur, India*
1404/1983	*Karachi, Pakistan*
1405/1984	*Nairobi, Kenya*
1406/1985	*Surat, India*
1407/1986	*Indore, India*
1408/1987	*Karachi, Pakistan*
1409/1988	*Mumbai, India*
1410/1989	*Surat, India*
1411/1990	*Dar-es-Salaam, Tanzania*
1412/1991	*Colombo, Sri Lanka*
1413/1992	*Pune, India*
1414/1993	*Mombasa, Kenya*
1415/1994	*Mumbai, India*
1416/1995	*Mombasa, Kenya*
1417/1996	*Karachi, Pakistan*
1418/1997	*Surat, India*
1419/1998	*Nairobi, Kenya*
1420/1999	*Colombo, Sri Lanka*
1421/2000	*Surat, India*

During the days of *'ashara*, there is no city, no town and no village where Dawoodi Bohras reside, however few in numbers, where gatherings are not held and where a *wā'iz* is not sent. Each of these centres is given the opportunity to hear a part of Syedna's discourse live by phone or internet through a well equipped radio and telephone arrangement.

A medical centre amidst the thousands is an essential requirement. Dawoodi Bohra doctors from different parts of the world volunteer their services and work with dedication to attend to the sick.

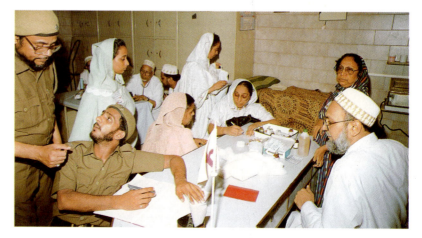

Sabīl al-Husain is the tradition of serving water, sometimes flavoured, to the grieving in the memory of Imām Husain's thirst. Seen here is *sabīl* arranged by the Bohra residents of Cairo, who set up elaborate *sabīl* centres each year.

Niyāz (food) served in the remembrance of Imām Husain is an essential part of the rites of remembrance. Thousands are fed within an hour or so, every partaker considering it a privilege to participate in the meal.

The love that is so much a part of the religion is also evidenced by Syedna's love and concern for his followers and their love and reverence for him. This relationship is best seen at a *qadambosi* gathering, in which individuals kiss Syedna's hand and avail the opportunity to narrate their most personal problems to their spiritual father. Every word of Syedna's advice is imbibed by his followers and often, one hears them recount how the course of their lives was altered by such advice. Syedna finds time to hold numerous such gatherings and attentively listens to each person, and then advises, consoles or shares the believer's grief or happiness.

Reciprocally, the Bohras revere Syedna and often display
this love openly. This was, for example, amply evident in
this march of solidarity in 1986 in Mumbai.

Pilgrimage to the shrines of the Prophet and his close family is one of the most potent ways of expressing love for them. The Bohras regularly perform the obligatory pilgrimage (*ḥajj*) to Makkah al-Mukarramah but visiting the shrines of their revered leaders is also a part of their religious tradition. Syedna Mohammed Burhanuddin has constructed tombs and sepulchres at such sites as a mark of esteem and love for them. Indeed, his first act on assuming the office of al-Dai al-Mutlaq in 1965 was to travel to Egypt for the dedication ceremony of the sepulchre of Rās al-Husain that was built by Syedna Taher Saifuddin. This act was indicative of the future as many more such dedications were to follow in his incumbency.

The Prophet is buried within the precincts of the great al-Masjid al-Nabawī in al-Madina al-Munawwara. Millions of Muslims from all over the world, including Bohras, visit the *masjid* every year to pay their respects to the benefactor of mankind and to pray at Islam's second most holy site (BELOW).

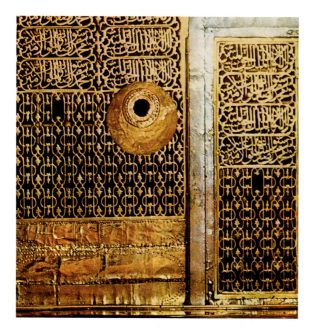

Bāb al-Mukhallafāt al-Nabawiyya al-Sharīfa, the silver portal within the martyrium of Imām Husain in Cairo is the entrance to a room that houses articles associated with the Prophet. Syedna built this portal and dedicated it in 1986 (ABOVE).

Ali ibn Abi Talib, the commander of the faithful and the successor of the Prophet, was martyred in Kufa and buried in Najaf al-Ashraf. Both are important sites of pilgrimage. Syedna Mohammed Burhanuddin built an ornate silver and gold portal at the site of Ali's martyrdom in the *masjid* in Kufa in 1974 (ABOVE RIGHT). In 1985, Syedna commissioned a gold overlay of the upper part of the sepulchre in Najaf, originally built by his father, the 51st *dā'ī*, in 1940.

The Rās al-Husain martyrium in Cairo, the final resting place of the sacred head of Imām Husain, is a site of pilgrimage for mourners, devotees and mystics. Its silver sepulchre was dedicated by Syedna Mohammed Burhanuddin in 1965 (RIGHT).

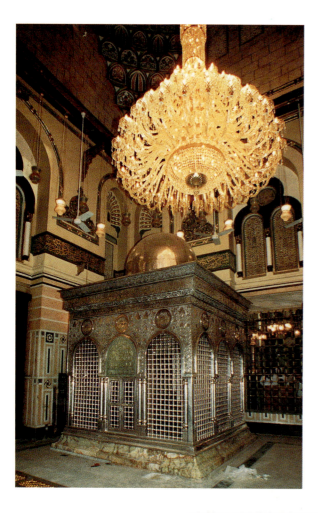

Sayyida Zaynab bint Ali, the sister of Imām Husain, braved the atrocities at Karbala and its aftermath. Her forbearance and courage inspire men and women alike. She is buried in Cairo, where her mausoleum attracts thousands of pilgrims every day. The *maqṣūra* over her grave was built by Syedna Mohammed Burhanuddin and dedicated in 1978.

BELOW LEFT Imām Husain's head was first kept in an area close to the burial place of Prophet Yahya (John the Baptist). This place is now within the precincts of al-Masjid al-Kabīr in Damascus. In 1993, Syedna marked the site with a silver and gold shrine.

BELOW In Damascus lies the tomb where the heads of seventy martyrs of Karbala are buried. In 1993, Syedna rebuilt the tomb and replaced its wooden shrine.

The shrines of Jafar ibn Abi Talib (LEFT) and Zayd ibn Haritha (RIGHT) in Jordan were built by Syedna and dedicated in 1999.

The *maqṣūra* of Ruqayyah bint Ali in Cairo was built and dedicated by Syedna in 1995.

Al-Hurrat al-Malika Arwa bint Ahmad, the celebrated 12th century queen of Yemen governed on behalf of the *imām* and was responsible for the appointment of the first *dāʿī* to serve as vicegerent during the *imām's* seclusion. Her grave lies alongside her *masjid* in Zi-Jibla. Syedna built the shrine surrounding her grave in 1994.

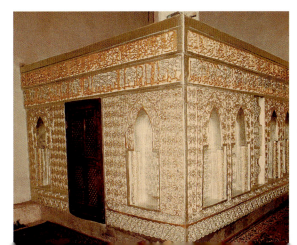

Restored 11th century Fatimi design.
Al-Anwar, Cairo.

AMBASSADOR OF GOODWILL

خَالِطُوا النَّاسَ مُخَالَطَةً

اِنْ عِشْتُمْ مَعَهَا حَنُّوْا اِلَيْكُمْ، وَاِنْ مُتُّمْ بَكَوْا عَلَيْكُمْ

'Mingle with people in such a way that as long as
you live they are drawn towards you, and when you
are no longer amidst them they weep for you.'

AMĪR AL-MU' MINĪN, ALI IBN ABI TALIB

'Goodwill missions from any country can be categorised into two kinds.
The first is through appointment to a ruling government for a fixed period
of time in which the appointed representative shoulders the government's
responsibilities and adheres to its rules during his tenure. The other
mission relates not to a post but a pledge — a pledge to Allah, to
humanity, to faith, to community and to country. It is an unwritten
pledge, it is allied to character and its influence is far-reaching. Its term
spans the life of the individual and the execution of the pledge is an
article of faith. I, like my predecessors and Syedna Taher Saifuddin in
particular, have acted according to this pledge and will do so forever.'

SYEDNA MOHAMMED BURHANUDDIN

AMBASSADOR OF GOODWILL

THE PLEDGE that great leaders make to themselves is to promote goodwill through a personal example of pristine character. This, as Syedna Mohammed Burhanuddin ﷺ often points out, is a part of faith. Such a mission requires an inner strength of conviction, a belief that the mission itself is worthwhile and a confidence in the ultimate goodness of humanity. Bonds have to be forged and what binds has to be developed over that which divides. Syedna has encouraged his followers to forge links that transcend barriers of race and religion and to remain faithful to the land of their abode as an article of their faith. He puts these teachings into practice by developing graciousness and congeniality with all who come in touch with him.

His mission is also carried out by his many travels. He uses these journeys as an opportunity to experience, observe and imbibe the diversity of Allah's creations and the variety of traditions, cultures and religions that make up the world.

The Dawoodi Bohra community is spread over the five continents. Though the largest numbers of Bohras live in India and Pakistan, significant communities exist in the Middle East, Yemen, East Africa, Madagascar, Sri Lanka, North America, France and United Kingdom. Smaller numbers reside all over the world, including countries of the Far East, Australia, Northern Europe and French speaking Africa. Syedna Mohammed Burhanuddin ﷺ has made it a mission to visit his followers wherever they may be. Whilst Bohras all over the world share the same beliefs and practices, and are equally dedicated and loyal to their leader, each community faces different challenges posed by the environment of its country. Syedna experiences such challenges first-hand by visiting his followers in the land of their abode and applies his insight into their wellbeing. He guides them towards adherence to their faith and establishes them as loyal, contributing citizens of the nations they have chosen to make their home. The effect of Syedna's presence amidst his community where they live is phenomenal. The community reaffirms its faith, has its dedications renewed and its communal institutions revitalised. Others welcome Syedna as an ambassador of goodwill and amity. As Syedna meets leaders and exchanges cordiality, the community he represents is established more firmly through its leader and is able to articulate its identity with greater confidence.

INDIA

India has been the home of the *dā'īs* for over half a millennium. Its spirit of tolerance is exemplified even in this century, for example, by the values expounded by the father of the nation, Mahatma Gandhi. The seat of the *da'wah* was first in Sidhpur. Later it moved to Ahmedabad, then Jamnagar, Mandvi, Ujjain, Burhanpur, Surat and is located today in Mumbai. Many sites important to the history and religion of the Bohras exist in India which is home to over six hundred thousand Bohras. Syedna has visited most of the many cities in India in which his followers reside.

Badri Mahal, a heritage building, located at Fort, Mumbai, houses the administrative offices of Dawat-e-Hadiyah.

Syedna's residence, Saifee Mahal, at Malabar Hill, Mumbai.

Mahatma Gandhi's Salt March ended at the foot of Syedna Taher Saifuddin's bungalow in Dandi, Gujarat, where he stayed during the uprising as a guest of Syedna Taher Saifuddin. The building was later dedicated to the nation and is today a museum of Mahatma Gandhi's life. Syedna Taher Saifuddin and Syedna Mohammed Burhanuddin with Colonel B.H. Zaidi at Rajghat, the memorial for Mahatma Gandhi in New Delhi.

India's first Prime Minister, Jawaharlal Nehru enjoyed a cordial relationship with Syedna Taher Saifuddin and they often met. Seen to the right, Jawaharlal Nehru dons a Bohra cap at a luncheon at the residence of Syedna Taher Saifuddin in Surat.

With the late Prime Minister Indira Gandhi.

INDIA

Al-Jamea-tus-Saifiyah houses a large library of rare books and manuscripts pertaining to the religion and history of the *da'wah*. Seen below, is Jawaharlal Nehru viewing some of the manuscripts during his visit to Al-Jamea-tus-Saifiyah in 1961.

Syedna Mohammed Burhanuddin with
past Presidents, Dr. S. Radhakrishnan
and Dr. Zakir Husain, both of who were
close friends of Syedna and the
community.

Past President Dr. Rajendra
Prasad is seen laying flowers at
the mausoleum of Syedna
Qutbuddin Shahid in
Ahmedabad in 1960.

INDIA

CLOCKWISE

With past Presidents, Dr. Fakhruddin Ali Ahmed, Mr. Sanjiva Reddy, Giani Zail Singh, and Dr. Shankar Dayal Sharma. President Giani Zail Singh is seen at the mausoleum of Syedna Taher Saifuddin in Mumbai which he visited in 1983.

Just as Syedna enhances the amity and brotherhood between India and other lands as he travels, he has often conducted the same role by inviting dignitaries to India.

In 1975, the community in India was host to the first ever gathering for the recitation of the Qur'an which renowned practitioners, such as Shaikh Mahmoud Khalil al-Huseri and Shaikh Abdul Basit attended (ABOVE).

At the same time, a colloquium on Islam and Arabic Studies was held in which Syedna spoke of the necessity of research and study being directed towards the benefit of all mankind (LEFT).

Syedna with Prince Karim Aga Khan IV during an early visit of the latter to India.

Syedna with leaders of Hindu and Sikh communities in Mumbai, India.

PAKISTAN

Syedna Taher Saifuddin's guidance to his
followers at the time of independence was to
ensure firm loyalty to their new nation wherever
partition found them. Today, about a hundred
thousand Dawoodi Bohras reside in Pakistan,
contributing to the nation's economic progress.

Syedna and his predecessor with
Mohammed Ali Jinnah in Mumbai
before independence.

Syedna visited the mausoleum of
Qaid-e-Azam in Karachi in one of
his official visits to Pakistan.

A quiet moment with President
Zia ul-Haq.

With President Field Marshal
Ayub Khan.

PAKISTAN

With past Prime Ministers, Mr. Zulfiqar Ali Bhutto and Mrs. Benazir Bhutto.

With General Parvez Musharraf, the present head of State.

At the inauguration of Al-Jamea-tus-Saifiyah, Karachi in 1983 with President Zia ul-Haq, Governor Abbasi and Mohammed Hasan al-Touhami of Egypt.

President Zia ul-Haq viewing a calligraphy exhibition set up by the academy.

'Islam is not a faith alone. It is an effective and complete code of life. Within it is the power latent to cast the whole of human society into one common mould. Its appeal is international.'

SYEDNA MOHAMMED BURHANUDDIN
At the inauguration of Al-Jamea-tus-Saifiyah,
Karachi on 5th November 1983.

SAUDI ARABIA

The *ḥajj*, pilgrimage to Makkah, is obligatory on every Muslim. Syedna has performed *ḥajj* five times. However, even when the journey is one of personal spiritual fulfilment, the opportunity to exchange cordiality within the brotherhood of Islam is not lost. Seen here, (TOP TO BOTTOM), is Syedna in the garb of a pilgrim, with King Saud ibn 'Abdul 'Azīz during the King's visit to India and King Faisal ibn 'Abdul 'Azīz during Syedna's visit to Saudi Arabia in 1969.

AL QUDS (Jerusalem)

Mentioned in the Qur'an, al-Masjid al-Aqṣā stands on sacred ground associated with prophets revered in Islam. It is also believed to be the place from which the Prophet ascended to the heavens (*mi'rāj*). It is considered the third holiest place in Islam.

With the Mufti of Jerusalem, Amin al-Husseini, in 1937.

Syedna supplicating in the area beneath the sacred rock in Masjid al-Ṣakhra, which is within the surrounds of al-Masjid al-Aqṣā.

JORDAN

With King Hussein al-Hashimi at the King's residence, in 1994.

With King Abdullah II al-Hashimi in 1999.

Syedna was conferred the "Star of Jordan – Class I", the highest civic honour of the country, in December 1981.

IRAQ

Whilst the holy cities of Makkah, Madina, and Al-Quds (Jerusalem) are considered by Muslims to be holy consecrated ground for prayer as well as sacred sites for pilgrimage, Najaf and Karbala, in which the hallowed shrines of the *Ahl al-Bayt* are located, are important pilgrimage sites to which Shī'a Muslims flock in their thousands every year.

BELOW Syedna with thousands of Bohras entering the shrine of Ali ibn Abi Talib in Najaf.

Recitation of a *salām* at the sepulchre of
Imām Husain in Karbala (ABOVE). During his
pilgrimage in 1994, he met Vice President of
Iraq, Mr. Ezzat Ibrahim (RIGHT) and the
Governor of Karbala (ABOVE RIGHT).

SYRIA

Supplication at the dedication ceremony of the sepulchre of Maqām Rās al-Husain (ABOVE) and with Syrian dignitaries at the dedication ceremony of sepulchre of Ru'ūs al-Shuhadā' (RIGHT), both in Damascus in 1993.

With President Hafez al-Asad at
the Presidential Palace.

Syed Ahmed Kaftaru, the Grand Mufti of
Syria is Syedna's close friend.

EGYPT

Egypt, the land of the Fatimi Imāms has a special place in the hearts of the Bohras. Syedna has often visited the land on pilgrimage, to build and renovate Fatimi monuments and to visit his followers living in Egypt.

Syedna with President Gamal Abdel Nasser in 1965.

With the Presidents Anwar Sadat and Hosni Mubarak. The latter presented the highest civic honour of Egypt, the "Order of the Nile" to Syedna in 1978.

'To attain eminence, undertake travel. Travel will attract five benefits: it will dispel sorrow, it will engender the earning of a livelihood, it will increase knowledge, it will enhance etiquette and it will provide the company of the noble.'

AMĪR AL-MU'MINĪN ALI IBN ABI TALIB

EGYPT

CLOCKWISE FROM LEFT
With Mohammed Hasan al-
Touhami, a scholar of distinction
and a close friend of Syedna; the
rector of Al-Azhar, Syed Ahmed
Hasan al-Baqoori and the
Shaikhul Azhar, Shaikh
Mohammad al-Fahham.

CLOCKWISE FROM ABOVE
Meetings with former prime ministers, Mr. Mohammed Saleem, Dr. Kamal al-Ganzouri and Dr. Mohammed Atef Sedki. Also with the late speaker of the parliament, Dr. Rifat al-Mahgub.

YEMEN

Yemen remained the seat of the *da'wah* for four centuries and is the land where the early *dā'īs* are buried. Syedna was the first incumbent to the office of al-Dai al-Mutlaq in India to have visited it. He restored the place of his followers in Yemen within the greater Bohra fraternity.

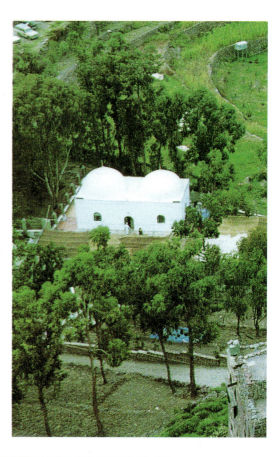

The tomb of Syedna Hatim, the 3rd *dā'ī*, on the mountainous al-Hutayb, a site that draws thousands of pilgrims throughout the year.

A view of al-Hutayb.

The President, Ali Abdullah Saleh, who has spoken of Syedna as the embodiment of Fatimi heritage.

A discussion with the late president, Sayyid Abd al-Rahman al-Iryani.

Syedna amidst his followers in Haraz, Yemen.

UNITED ARAB EMIRATES

The Bohras have settled in the Emirates, Kuwait, Muscat and Bahrain since the 1940s. Many have set up successful businesses that have contributed to the economies of the countries. In Dubai and Bahrain, the community has built *masjids* where they perform their religious duties.

Syedna with Shaikh Zayed bin Sultan al Nahyan, President of U.A.E. and Ruler of Abu Dhabi.

With the late Shaikh Rashid bin Saeed al-Maktoum, the Vice President of U.A.E. and Ruler of Dubai.

President meets Bohra leader

President His Highness Sheikh Zayed bin Sultan al Nahyan yesterday received Bohra leader Dr. Syedna Mohammed Burhanuddin at Al Mushrif Palace. At the 40-minute meeting they discussed a number of issues connected with Islamic affairs and the welfare of the Muslims in general. Dr Burhanuddin praised the wise and benevolent leadership of the President and the farsightedness in undertaking projects for the welfare and development of the country and the help extended by him to all Islamic countries in the world. The significance behind Sheikh Zayed's deep interest in Islamic affairs and the establishment of Quranic centres under the Zayed Project for Recitation and Memorisation of Holy Quran all over the UAE was appreciated by Dr Burhanuddin. The President was briefed about the mosque built by the Dawoodi Bohra community in Dubai. The President expressed happiness at the contribution made by the Bohra community in various fields of education, commerce and industry in the country. Present at the meeting were Ahmed Khalifa al Suweidi, the President's Representative. Dr Burhanuddin made a presentation to Sheikh Zayed.

WAM photo

KUWAIT

With the Amir of Kuwait,
Shaikh Jabir al-Sabah (TOP)
and Crown Prince Shaikh
Saad al-Abdullah (BELOW).

BANGLADESH

About a thousand Bohras live in Bangladesh. Syedna visited the country in 1992, when he met the President, Abdul Rahman Biwas and the Prime Minister, Mrs Begum Khalida.

SRI LANKA

The Bohra community in Sri Lanka is small but entrepreneurial. It is known to have some of the best businessmen in the country. Syedna has often visited the congregation and inspired them to run their vast businesses in accordance with Islam.

Seen here with Syedna is the late President, Mr. J.R. Jayewardene (BELOW) and the late Prime Minister, Mr. Premadasa (LEFT).

In a message to the delegates to the *International Seminar on the Universality of Islam* held in Colombo in 1982, Syedna emphasised that not only is it incumbent upon a Muslim to practice Islam for his own betterment and success, he must also use the teachings of Islam in the service of humanity as a whole. He also said that the Muslim must acknowledge the universality of the *shari'ah* and demonstrate its practicality by its application on oneself.

KENYA

Syedna makes it his duty to travel to his followers. In East Africa where they have settled for over a century, the community has grown and flourished, contributing substantially to its nations. Syedna first visited Kenya and Tanzania with his predecessor in 1963 and has since returned often. He is welcomed as a state guest and often meets leaders of the nation as well as communities with whom his followers live and interact.

A meeting with President Daniel Arap Moi in 1980.

'The Islamic society is the source from which flows the means for the welfare and wellbeing of mankind, irrespective of faith and creed. For Allah has decreed that every Muslim shall strive to benefit Allah's creation as a whole. This obligation has been made in successive verses and the expectations from an Islamic society expressly propounded. Islamic society, as Allah willed, should be perfect, strong and successful by benefiting the entirety of mankind.'

SYEDNA MOHAMMED BURHANUDDIN
Muslim Association of Mombasa conference, 1980.

TANZANIA

With President Ali Hasan
Mwinyi in 1990.

During Syedna's visit to Tanzania in 1984, the local community
had organised a function to celebrate *Mīlād al-Nabī*, the birth
anniversary of the Prophet, which was attended by then Vice-
President Ali Hasan Mwinyi and other state dignitaries.

With Prime Minister Salim Ahmed
Salim (ABOVE) and the President of
Zanzibar, Idris Abdul Wakil in 1990.

MADAGASCAR

CLOCKWISE

Syedna with Professor Albert Zafy, President of High State Authority in Madagascar and Didier Ratsiraka, President of Madagascar and Prime Minister Mr. Gol Willy in 1992. The Prime Minister sought Syedna's prayer for rains in the drought-stricken country and remarked that Allah would surely answer Syedna's intercession. A heavy downpour during Syedna's stay in the country made headlines, addressing Syedna as "The Rainmaker".

USA AND CANADA

There are about six thousand Dawoodi Bohras resident in the USA and Canada. The community in North America is organised into twenty-three centres, each having its own community centre. Dallas, Detroit, Houston and Toronto have *masjids*. Syedna has visited his followers in North America several times over the last twenty-five years. In each visit, he has been welcomed by governors and other officials of the states and cities and been accorded accolades and honours. In 1996, for example, he was given honorary citizenship of Houston in Texas and San Jose in California.

Members of the community residing in Houston meet President Clinton, June 2000.

'You live in a country that is progressive and technologically advanced; a country that took man to the moon and returned him safely back to earth. I am pleased to know that living amidst such worldly progress and scientific advancement has not weakened your belief in religion, and your faith in the Creator of the Heavens and Earth is unmoved.'

SYEDNA MOHAMMED BURHANUDDIN
addressing Muslims at the Islamic Centre of Detroit, 22nd October 1978.

UNITED KINGDOM

In 1976, Muslim scholars and activists from all over the world met in London to host the "World of Islam Festival", an ambitious programme to highlight the message of Islam and the rich cultural tradition that Islam had fostered. Syedna was invited to address the gathering at its inauguration ceremony, at which he said that it is the task of Muslims "to bring out the qualities of Islam to lighten the burdens that humanity is enduring in the East and the West – of disharmony and disunity, the pangs of hunger and poverty and the forces of destruction…."

Excerpts from an address by Syedna Mohammed Burhanuddin, at the International Islamic Conference on Aspects of Islamic Studies, 5th April, 1976:

'If ever there was a book which inspired a community, delivered it from the wilderness, and emancipated it to a life of higher values, idealism and honour, and forged the political, social and intellectual history of mankind, – that book without doubt, is the noble Qur'an. Its impact on the Muslims in material and spiritual life is certain…..

Then, quoting Ali ibn Abi Talib, he said:

"The Qur'an is Light from Allah. A mercy vouchsafed to us. It is guidance in the wilderness of life. It is a cure for doubting hearts and illusions of the soul. It is a criterion between verity and error. It contains manifest signs which will never lead its followers to perdition. It is an insight which reveals the mysteries of creation. It is good tidings for the world. It is spirit emanating from Allah's command…."

'Let us listen to the Qur'an with open hearts.'

Syedna visits UK at least once a year. His community in UK, numbering about three thousand, has benefited immensely from his numerous visits and established a neighbourhood around their *masjid* in Northolt, Middlesex.

An introduction with Queen Elizabeth II in 1976 when Syedna had visited London as the guest of the organisers of the "World of Islam Festival".

In the Mohammedi Park complex in Northolt, Middlesex, lies the grave of Amatullah Aaisaheba, the revered wife of Syedna. The Prince of Wales visited the complex in 1996.

Dawat-e-Hadiyah Act 1993   c. x   1

ELIZABETH II

1993   CHAPTER x

An Act to incorporate the Dai al-Mutlaq as a corporation sole; and for related purposes.
[1st July 1993]

WHEREAS His Holiness Dr. Syedna Mohammed Burhanuddin is the fifty-second incumbent in the office of the Dai al-Mutlaq, having been duly appointed by an act of designation in accordance with the canons and principles of the mission known as Dawat-e-Hadiyah:

And whereas the Dai al-Mutlaq is the supreme head of Dawat-e-Hadiyah and its people professing Islam distinguished as the Shiah Fatimi Ismaili Tayyibi Dawoodi Bohras known as the Dawoodi Bohra Community:

And whereas Dawat-e-Hadiyah promotes and fosters the interests of the Dawoodi Bohra Community:

The Parliament of Great Britain and Northern Ireland enacted the Dawat-e-Hadiyah Act 1993 recognising al-Dai al-Mutlaq as a corporation sole.

Syedna Mohammed Burhanuddin

EPILOGUE

The greatest bounty that man receives is the guidance that illuminates his path to the hereafter. A fulfilled life is one that multiplies this bounty by its own endeavour. The worth of such a life is inestimable and the span of its influence, infinite.

Let this narration end, then, with the praise of Allah, Lord of the Worlds.

O You who I worship!
My thankfulness is insignificant before your great boons,
And my praise and my declarations of gratitude pale before your generosity.
Your favours have wrapped me in robes of the lights of faith,
And the gentlenesses of your good have covered me with a delicate curtain of might.
Your kindnesses have given me a strength that cannot be shaken
And adorned me with dignities that cannot be broken.
Your boons are abundant
And my tongue too weak to count them.
Your favours are many
My understanding falls short of grasping them, let alone exhausting them.
So how can I truly be thankful?
When my thanking You requires thanksgiving.
Whenever I say "To You belongs praise"
It becomes thereby incumbent upon me to say,
"To You belongs praise."

From a supplication of thankfulness by the 3rd *imām*,
ALI IBN AL-HUSAIN, ZAIN AL-ABIDIN .

GLOSSARY OF SELECTED TERMS

Ahl al-Bayt Literally "people of the house (of the Prophet)", a term used to describe the Prophet Mohammed ﷺ and his immediate family consisting of his successor Ali, his daughter Fatima who was married to Ali, and Hasan and Husain, the two sons of Ali and Fatima. The term also describes the *imāms* from the progeny of Husain. The love of *Ahl al-Bayt* is a cornerstone of the Fatimi faith adhered to by the Dawoodi Bohras.

ʿamil The leader of the local congregation (*jamāʿat*) of the Bohras, appointed by Syedna.

ʿĪd al-fiṭr The festival that marks the end of Ramaḍān, the month in which Muslims fast daily.

ʿaqīqa The sacrifice performed on the 7th, 14th or 21st day after the birth of a child. It is an important Islamic rite.

ʿashara The 9 days prior to and including 'Āshūrā' during which gatherings are held in every Bohra centre all over the world in remembrance of the martyrdom of Imām Husain.

ʿĀshūrā' The 10th day of Muḥarram, the first month of the Muslim calendar. The day on which the martyrdom of *Imām* Husain occurred.

dāʿī Literally, "summoner", appointed by the *imām* to summon people to religion. It is an abbreviated term for ranks such as *dāʿī al-balāgh* and *al-dāʿī al-muṭlaq* operating during Fatimi empire, as well as for the position of *dāʿī al-muṭlaq* that represents the *imām* during his seclusion.

al-dāʿī al-muṭlaq (al-Dai al-Mutlaq) Literally "summoner with comprehensive authority", a rank in the religious hierarchy designated by the *imām*. When the *imām* enters seclusion, the al-Dai al-Mutlaq leads the mission on the *imām*'s behalf, as the *imām*'s representative and vicegerent.

al-duʿāt al-muṭlaqīn Plural of *al-dāʿī al-muṭlaq*.

ḥajj The annual pilgrimage to Makkah al-Mukarramah, that is one of the foundational practices of Islam.

imām The descendant of the Prophet who leads and guides the faithful, and whose existence in each age, and whose guidance is believed to be necessary for salvation.

jamāʿat The organisation that oversees the affairs of a local congregation.

khuṭba Literally, "sermon" or "discourse", specially delivered during the Friday prayers and considered to be an integral part of prayer.

lisān al-daʿwah The language employed by the Dawoodi Bohras, which is essentially based on Gujarati, but with a script and a large part of the vocabulary being Arabic.

madrasa Literally school, but usually used to describe a school of religious education.

majlis The formal gathering which has a set etiquette, and in which socio-religious ceremonies are conducted and a discourse delivered.

maqṣūra An ornate surrounding, often made of silver and gold, installed around a burial place, and considered as being blessed. Also called *ḍarīḥ*, and translated as sepulchre.

masjid Mosque. Literally, a place where prostration is performed, the *masjid* is a place of worship, and the centre of all religious and educational activities of the Muslim community.

miḥrāb Prayer niche in the *masjid*, in which the one who leads the communal prayer, prays.

mīṣāq The covenant with Allah and an oath of allegiance to the al-Dai al-Mutlaq, entered into by every Bohra on reaching adolescence.

munājāt A pleading prayer written in metered poetry, for the occasion of Laylat al-Qadr, the holiest night of the Muslim calendar, falling on the 23rd of Ramaḍān.

muqarnas An architectural niched design, often calligraphic, that forms an emblem that is ornamental yet architecturally significant to the building.

musāfirkhāna A rest house commonly located close to a place of pilgrimage. The rest house provides free or subsidised accommodation and food to the pilgrims.

nikāḥ Marriage according to Islamic rites, particularly the ceremony of making vows.

qadambosi The kissing of the hand (and sometimes knees) as a mark of respect. Bohra children do this to their parents and elders but the term applies mainly to the kissing of the hand of Syedna, which is considered an honour by Bohras.

qarḍan ḥasanā Literally, "a good loan", praised in the Qu'ran. Commonly understood to be an interest-free loan.

ribā' Interest charged on lending of money, that is forbidden in Islam. Sometimes translated as usury to denote that it is only forbidden in

its exploitative nature, though this interpretation is now discredited.

ridā' The all-covering dress worn by Bohra women. It comes in two sections, one covering the head, arms and upper body, and the other, like a long dress, worn at the waist to cover the lower part of the body. It need not be plain, nor of dark colour – most are light coloured and patterned.

sabaq A method of teaching religious lore that goes as far back as 14 centuries.

salām A salutation and tribute read at the tombs of the Prophet and the *Ahl al-Bayt*.

satr Literally "seclusion", a term used to describe the state of the *imām* when he retires from public view and conducts his mission through his vicegerent, the *dā'ī*. The Dawoodi Bohras believe that all *imāms* from the 21st have chosen to remain in *satr*.

sharī'ah The body of law that comprises all actions and religious ordinance. Dawoodi Bohras adhere to the Fatimi school of thought, which requires belief in 7 principles (*da'ā'im*) of Islam, these being *walāyah* (love and devotion to the Prophet, the *imāms* and their *dā'īs*), *ṭahārah* (purity and cleanliness), *salāh* (prayer), *zakāh* (religious due), *ṣawm* (fasting in the month of Ramaḍān), *ḥajj* (pilgrimage to Makkah) and *jihād* (striving against the lower self and protection of the cause).

taqwā A sense of fear and love of Allah that is considered to be the essence of the complex relationship between man and Allah.

tawḥīd Belief in the oneness of Deity. This is the cardinal principle of monotheism and fundamental to all Islamic beliefs.

topi A white cap with gold border that is worn by Dawoodi Bohra men.

ummah A single community to which all Muslims belong.

wālī One appointed by the *dā'ī* living in Yemen (during the 12th to 16th centuries) to manage the affairs of the *da'wah* in India. Literally "one who is authorised".

waṣī The one chosen by the Prophet to succeed him and interpret religious doctrine after him. A rank in the religious hierarchy second only to the Prophet, and occupied by the Prophet's son-in-law Ali ibn Abi Talib.

zakāh The religious due paid by Muslims each year, that is part of the cardinal principles of the *sharī'ah*.

ziyārah A visitation to a sacred place, often the place of burial of the Prophet and his immediate family. Also written *ziyārat*.

TRANSLITERATION TABLE

Arabic letter	Transliteration
ء	ʾ
ب	b
ت	t
ث	ṣ
ج	j
ح	ḥ
خ	kh
د	d
ذ	ẓ
ر	r
ز	z
س	s
ش	sh
ص	ṣ
ض	ḍ
ط	ṭ
ظ	ẓ
ع	ʿ
غ	gh
ف	f
ق	q
ك	k
ل	l
م	m
ن	n
ه	h
و	w
ي	y
ة	t, h or omitted

Short vowels

َ	a
ُ	u
ِ	i

Long vowels

ا	ā
و	ū
ي	ī

Dipthongs

وْ	aw
يْ	ay
ـِ يّ	iyy
ـُ وّ	uw w